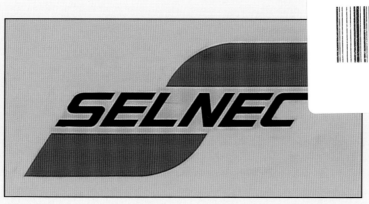

- a 40th Celebration . . .

To
Peter Horton

D Scott Hellewell

D Scott Hellewell

Venture *publications*

© 2009 Venture Publications Ltd

ISBN 978 1905 304 33 2

Computer Origination, Design and Layout by John and Mark Senior

This book has been written to celebrate the 40th anniversary of the establishment of the South East Lancashire and North East Cheshire Passenger Transport Authority and Executive (SELNEC PTA and PTE) on 1st November 1969. SELNEC, based in Manchester, was the largest of the four original PTEs. Although it only existed 4½ years (being subsumed into Greater Manchester PTA/PTE) it had a major influence on Britain's public transport, especially buses. The foundations of some of today's developments were laid in those days and many of the people involved went on to greater heights in the passenger transport industry.

The arrival of the brightly painted orange and white buses marked perhaps the biggest change the city had seen since the withdrawal of the trams in 1949. Twenty years on, with the formation of **SELNEC**, great changes were to take place. Even greater changes would take place in the next 20 years with de-regulation in 1986 being followed by privatisation of bus operation with a whole host of operators and liveries taking to the streets. Former Manchester Mancunian 1042 coming into the city from Worsley passes the Central Library and marks what many would consider as a stable and well-organised period of Manchester's transport history. *(STA)*

In Earlier Times

The formation of SELNEC in 1969 was a significant event, integrating all public transport in what we now call the Greater Manchester area. There had been an earlier proposal, in 1932, to form such an organisation – The South East Lancashire Joint Board – but at that time there was not the will between all the local authorities as they considered the implications to their own finances and influence and it took the foresight and politcal clout of Blackburn Labour MP Barbara Castle in a Labour Government with a strong majority in Parliament to provide the legislation by the passing of the 1968 Transport Act.

SELNEC was thus set up as a political animal and in its short life, between 1969 and 1974, it did what most people will concede was a good job in integrating the area's transport network. Along the way it acquired the former BET operator North Western, with one segment becoming SELNEC Cheshire in 1972, it bought the largest independent operator, Lancashire United Transport (LUT), and later embraced Wigan when the Boundary Changes brought that operator into its area in 1974. Thereafter the mantle was taken on by its successor – Greater Manchester Transport – until in 1985 Margaret Thatcher's Conservative Goverment wrecked the whole scheme, under her lieutenant, Nicholas Ridley, forcing the deregulation and subsequent privatisation which will long be remembered for years of streets full of smokey old buses carrying few passengers.

However, it should also be remembered that as far back as 1880 the area had been served by one private operator of horse buses and trams – The Manchester Carriage and Tramway Company Ltd.

This organisation had at its maximum over 600 vehicles and a stud of some 5,244 horses. It operated as far as Stockport in the south, Peel Green in the west, Stalybridge in the east and Oldham in the north. Its route mileage was an impressive 143 miles.

Under the terms of the 1870 Tramways Act local authorities were empowered to compulsorily purchase the horse tramway lines after 21 years, and since the boom years for the Manchester Company had been between 1877 and 1883 the various 21-leases expired around the turn of the century. It is for this reason that some of our various local municipalities began their electric tramcar operation between 1899 (Bolton) and 1904 (Rochdale).

Providing sufficient power for the new electric trams required generating stations to be built, and supply and distribution arrangments made. Buses at this time were in their infancy and with the exception of Ramsbottom which introduced trolleybuses in 1913 electric trams were the staple people movers until buses became more reliable. At first the fledgling buses were used as feeders but gradually their role

From 1824 public transport in the Manchester area had been provided by horse buses, then from 1877 by horse trams and from 1899 to 1951 by electric trams. Examples of all three types of vehicle are seen here in an operating session in Manchester's Heaton Park on a fine day in 2008. The horse-drawn vehicles were originally owned by the Manchester Carriage and Tramway Company, the electric tram by the Corporation. (JAS)

THE SELNEC OPERATING AREA

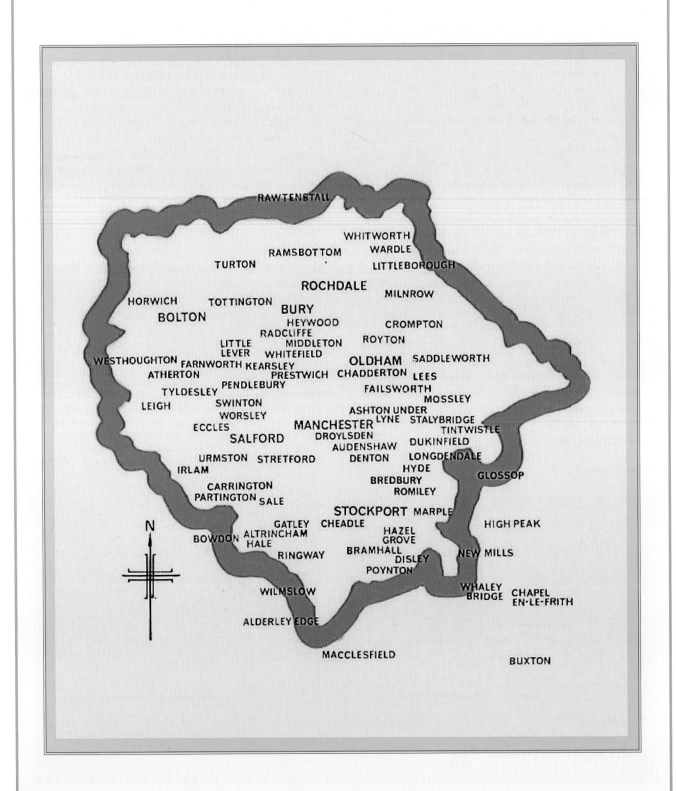

FROM THE BIGGEST . . .

Manchester City Transport was the largest constituent of SELNEC PTE, providing 1220 buses. The Bennett 'Mancunian' design had been introduced in 1968 and was built on Leyland Atlantean and Daimler Fleetline chassis. Here No. 2058 on a Fleetline chassis is seen in Cateaton Street, passing the Corn Exchange on service 19 from Victoria Station to Reddish (Holdsworth Square). Manchester Cathedral can be seen in the middle distance. This area has been transformed by redevelopment following the IRA bomb destruction. The ever-popular Morris Minor van and a Ford Anglia car represent the only competition for the one-man-operated bus. *(JAS)*

The smallest undertaking vested in SELNEC was Ramsbottom Urban District Council's fleet of 12 buses. Ramsbottom was incorporated into the Bury District of the Northern Division. Number 11 of the Ramsbottom fleet, now 6411 in SELNEC days, was the last Leyland Titan PD3 to be built for the home market. It is an East Lancashire Coachbuilders' double-decker with forward entrance and is now preserved, in original livery, in the Manchester Museum of Transport at Boyle Street, Cheetham Hill, Manchester along with representatives of the fleets which passed to SELNEC, and others. *(DSH)*

. . . TO THE SMALLEST

After receiving its first Atlanteans Salford had kept its options open by taking further examples of Leyland front-engined models such as this PD2 seen at the Kingsway terminus of the 95 service. Conductor-operation was still the norm and the move to forward entrances was in line with passenger safety where the driver could supervise loading and unloading. Examples of Manchester's Mancunian and earlier Leyland PD2 models can be seen in the distance. (JAS)

was extended and in 1929, after the death of Manchester's manager Henry Mattinson, his replacement – from Edinburgh – R Stuart Pilcher showed the industry that the days of the trams were numbered and he made the major tram to motorbus conversion of the famous 53 route in 1930. He very relucantly accepted trolleybuses in 1938 when overruled by the City Council.

Through-running and joint operation of the many trams had been possible thanks to far-sighted and sensible co-operation between undertakings – some more so than others – and the legacy of this widespread joint working was to provide SELNEC with a good solid working foundation. The importance of the joint operation of the trams, and the later buses and trolleybuses, cannot be overstressed. The accompanying table shows the impressive extent to which operators worked together to provide effecient and co-ordinated transport – without Government intervention!

OPERATOR	JOINTLY LICENSED WITH
ASHTON	MANCHESTER, NWRC, OLDHAM, ROCHDALE, SHMD, STOCKPORT
BOLTON	BURY, LEIGH, LUT, SALFORD
BURY	BOLTON, LUT, MANCHESTER, RAMSBOTTOM, ROCHDALE, SALFORD
LUT	BOLTON, BURY, LEIGH, NWRC, SALFORD, WIGAN
LEIGH	BOLTON, LUT, SALFORD
MANCHESTER	ASHTON, BURY, NWRC, OLDHAM, ROCHDALE, SHMD, SALFORD, STOCKPORT
NORTH WESTERN	ASHTON, LUT, MANCHESTER, OLDHAM, ROCHDALE, SHMD, STOCKPORT
OLDHAM	ASHTON, MANCHESTER, NWRC, ROCHDALE, SHMD
RAMSBOTTOM	BURY
ROCHDALE	ASHTON, BURY, MANCHESTER, NWRCC, OLDHAM
SHMD	ASHTON, MANCHESTER, NWRC, OLDHAM, STOCKPORT
SALFORD	BOLTON, BURY, LUT, LEIGH, MANCHESTER
STOCKPORT	ASHTON, MANCHESTER, NWRC, SHMD
WIGAN	LUT
ALTHOUGH OPERATORS HELD JOINT LICENSES WITH EACH OTHER, NOT ALL PARTIES NECESSARILY OPERATED VEHICLES ON THE SERVICES CONCERNED	

SELNEC CENTRAL

At Strangeways Magistrates' Court recently, a youth was fined £5 plus £4 costs for maliciously damaging a bus window.

Printed by Warburtons (Printers) Ltd., 35a Old Mill St., Manchester 4. Tel.: COL 4196   3248

Stockport, on the other hand, had remained faithful to the traditional front-engined configuration, using both PD2 and the longer PD3 models from Leyland, as here with number 73 at Hazel Grove. The presence of the emergency escape window in the bay behind the driver's cab is the distinguishing point between the PD3s and the shorter PD2s. Stockport narrowly escaped the rear engined problems when a batch of ten Bristol VR chassis and their bodies were badly damaged in a disastrous fire at East Lancashire Coachbuilders, its long-time preferred body maker. Although some chassis survived, the opportunity was taken to allow the manufacturer to find alternative homes for them. In due course, in SELNEC days, North Western would receive Bristol VRs with Eastern Coach Works bodies. *(DSH)*

Scenes like this were soon to be a thing of the past once the grand repainting into corporate livery was underway. Stevenson Square is host to Rochdale, Manchester and Oldham vehicles, the former, now renumbered as SELNEC Northern 6212, being one of Mr Franklin's famous AECs many of which were fitted with Gardner engines, and using the Manchester style destination display – but properly dressed. Untidy blind settings were legendary in Manchester. Until 1966 trolleybuses had also used this square as their terminus. *(STA)*

Oldham Corporation had been a long-time purchaser of bodywork from Roe in Leeds. Number 389, seen above in Ashton bus station, carries the Pommard livery introduced in 1966 and retained until **SELNEC** colours were applied. The original madder and white is shown on number 394, below, preserved in the Boyle Street collection and seen here whilst working the erstwhile Park Service in Manchester's Heaton Park. A former Stockport PD3 can been seen behind the trees, also working on this service. The earlier livery, below, highlights the traditional Roe teak waistrail; there had been an unsuccessful attempt to change to light blue and white but in the event Pommard was selected. *(DSH; JAS)*

Oldham was not alone in making substantial livery changes. When Charles Baroth took over as Salford's Manager in 1946 he changed the livery from red and white to green and cream. The pre-war livery is shown on the preserved Park Royal-bodied AEC in Boyle Street, top right, and this vehicle, built in 1939, survived into SELNEC ownership as a dual-control driver trainer. It passed into preservation in 1972. By 1946 Salford's fleet was very run down with buses and trams in wartime brown or red and brown. A massive intake of new vehicles took place and for many years the standard Salford bus was the Daimler CVG6 with Metro-Cammell 54-seat bodywork as seen at centre. Some 48 of these passed to SELNEC. *(JAS both)*

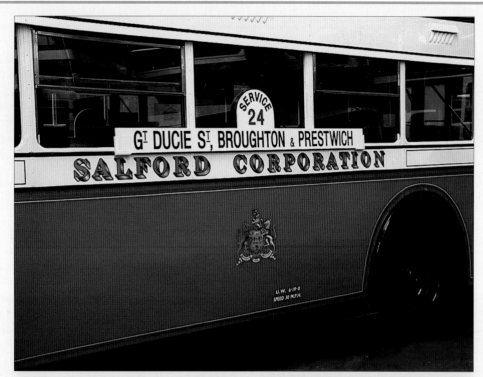

Leigh shared some features with North Western – both had a need for low height double-deckers, both took AEC Renowns to resolve the problem, and both also took Dennis Lolines for the same reason. Here we see Leigh Renown No. 15, by now preserved and restored to its former attractive livery, operating an enthusiasts' service from its Boyle Street, Manchester Museum of Transport, home. The attractive bodywork is by East Lancashire Coachbuilders of Blackburn. *(STA)*

Why, How, and By Whom?

SELNEC was the largest of the four original PTEs. The acronym stood for *South East Lancashire North East Cheshire* and was the then euphemism for Greater Manchester. The Passenger Transport Authorities (PTAs), the Political body, and their Executives (PTEs) were established by Order under Section 9 of the Transport Act 1968 – and thus national as opposed to local policy – and were to be responsible for integrating public transport in their areas. This meant integrating one bus operator with another, integrating buses and trains and integration with land-use planning. Each of these elements was a major job in itself; that the three had to be progressed simultaneously with a requirement to produce a policy statement within a year and a Development Plan within two years was a considerable work load. That SELNEC achieved these goals was a significant achievement in itself.

The other three PTEs were, in declining order of size, West Midlands, focussed on Birmingham, Merseyside, focussed on Liverpool, and Tyneside, focussed on Newcastle. Subsequently West Midlands was to incorporate Coventry; Tyneside became Tyne & Wear and incorporated Sunderland; SELNEC became Greater Manchester and included Wigan but lost the areas around Wilmslow and Glossop. Greater Glasgow (subsequently Strathclyde) PTE followed in 1973. South and West Yorkshire PTEs came in 1974.

The SELNEC (Designation) Order 1969 came into operation on 10th February 1969. The Passenger Transport Authority (PTA) – the policy-making body – consisted of 30 members: 26 representing local authorities that made up the SELNEC area and four nominated by the Minister of Transport. Fifteen members represented the County or County Borough Councils. Whilst the City of Manchester had the greatest number of members, it could not act without the support of at least two other councils.

Alderman Harry Sharp, former Chairman of Manchester's Transport Committee, was elected the first Chairman of the PTA. Sir Leonard Cooke was appointed Vice-Chairman. He was a member of the London Midland Railway Board and a member of the North West Economic Planning Council. The Town Clerk of Manchester acted as the Clerk to the PTA, the first meeting of which took place towards the end of April 1969. The members of the SELNEC PTA are shown on the inside rear cover. The appointment of the Director General and the other Directors followed

shortly thereafter. Following their appointment the Directors had a busy time deciding the principles upon which the organisation was to operate, the key management appointments, establishment of banking arrangements and transitional matters.

Overnight on 1st November 1969 SELNEC PTE became responsible for the operation of 2,514 buses, the largest bus organisation in the country outside London, which at the time ran about 6,000 buses. The PTE took over the municipal operations of Bolton, which had 249 buses; Bury (96); Rochdale (129); Oldham (185): Stalybridge, Hyde, Mossley and Dukinfield Joint Board (SHMD) (88); Ashton-under-Lyne (59); Leigh (57) and Stockport (148), together with the City fleets of Manchester (1,220) and Salford (271). Also included was the fleet of Ramsbottom Urban District Council (12), one of the many small municipal bus operators in Lancashire. SELNEC inherited 26 garages and workshops. In management terms the bus operations spanned from one of the smallest fleets, Ramsbottom with 12 buses, to one of the largest, Manchester, with over 1,200 buses. At the time the two-door Mancunian double-decker cost £10,800 and a single-door version cost £300 less. The General Managers of the Undertakings taken over are shown at the end of this section.

The population of the SELNEC area was 2.65m people and they lived in 64 local authorities. In addition to the two cities and five County Boroughs which ran the buses, there were parts of four Counties: the West Riding of Yorkshire, Derbyshire, Lancashire and Cheshire. There were 17 Municipal Boroughs, six of which ran buses, and four Rural District Councils. The area covered was roundly 545 square miles.

On Vesting Day on 1st November 1969 SELNEC's immediate job was to keep the vast route network running, to collect the fares and to pay the salaries and wages of 10,000 people. SELNEC buses carried 579m passengers per annum, the fleet operated 75m vehicle-miles and earned £30.4m annually.

There had been a long history of joint working agreements between some of the municipalities, and also between some of the municipalities and the company operators. The integration of these operations under the PTE's umbrella was a major challenge if the operational anomalies were to be removed and the economies of scale achieved. Not least of these achievements, over time, was the establishment of common farescales and ticketing arrangements across the whole of SELNEC.

Furthermore, the policies pursued by individual municipalities regarding finance, fares, operating and engineering matters etc often varied substantially. This reflected, in part, the Political views of the respective Councils, and, in part, the geographic and economic circumstances of the individual authorities.

Prior to the PTE, the terms and conditions of employment of the staff were agreed by the appropriate committee of the Municipal Passenger Transport Association (MPTA) and pay was also negotiated nationally. In the 1960s some of the larger municipalities opted out of the MPTA to allow them to pay higher wages to recruit and retain staff. Manchester was one such case. Every municipality had local agreements covering a multitude of matters relating to schedules, working practices and the conversion to omo. The establishment of the PTEs required these matters to be addressed with urgency and SELNEC's personnel staff had their work cut out developing company-wide pay, terms and conditions and negotiating these with the relevant trade unions. Initially the PTE was organised into three Divisions:

Northern, based in Bradshawgate, Bolton, and including Leigh, Bury, Rochdale and Ramsbottom. A total of 545 buses; 496 double-deckers and 49 single-deckers operating out of eight garages.

Central, based in Devonshire Street, Manchester, and including Salford. A total of 1493 vehicles; 1406 double-deckers and 88 single-deckers operating out of nine garages.

Southern, based in Daw Bank, Stockport and including Oldham, SHMD and Ashton. A total of 488 vehicles; 448 double-deckers and 40 single-deckers operating out of five garages.

The Divisional organisation consisted of a Divisional Manager, Divisional Traffic Manager, Divisional Engineer, Divisional Accountant and Divisional Personnel Officer. The Divisional Managers, who were also Associate Directors of the Executive, were JB (Jim) Batty for the Northern,　J (Jack) Thompson for Central and HN (Norman) Kay for the Southern.

Underneath the Divisional level was a District Structure with each of the former municipalities forming a District headed by a Manager and Traffic, Engineering and Personnel Managers. Ramsbottom was subsumed into Bury. SHMD and Ashton were combined and later became Tameside District; it was to be several years before the new garage was built there.

The Central Division was further sub-divided into three Areas: North Western based on Frederick Road garage, Salford; Eastern Area based on Devonshire Street and Southern Area based on Princess Road garage. Advisory Committees were established for the Northern and Southern Divisions and for each of the three Central Areas. The Directors and senior staff of SELNEC PTE are shown on page 16.

In addition to operating the former municipal fleets the Executives were responsible for the provision of other bus and rail services in their areas and for the planning of the future integrated transport networks. As Barbara Castle, the Minister of Transport, had said when promoting the Transport Act 1968, they needed to be staffed by 'men of vision', clearly implying a new start to public transport. The PTA/PTE concept had been observed by her in Hamburg, Stockholm, Boston (Massachusetts Bay Transportation Authority [MBTA]) and Toronto.

The concept of PTAs/PTEs was designed very much with (Greater) Manchester in mind and to be led by Manchester's charismatic General Manager, RF (Ralph) Bennett. He had moved to MCT in 1960 (having previously been at Bolton for five years) and succeeded AF (Albert) Neal who, in turn was appointed as Bus Adviser to Barbara Castle. In the event Ralph Bennett was persuaded by her to take over as Chairman of London Transport. SELNEC was the second of the PTEs to be established on 1st November 1969, West Midlands having been established on 1st October that year. Then followed Merseyside PTE on 1st December and Tyneside PTE, the smallest of the original four, on 1st January, 1970.

Editorial content in November 1969's *Bus and Coach* said: 'Undoubtedly the most complex task, both in term of numbers of undertakings absorbed and in the complexity of non-operating local authorities within its area, lies before SELNEC PTE .... Early signs are that the Executive will take the least orthodox line .... A clue to a different approach from the other PTE structures lies in the relatively self-contained management organisation.'

The SELNEC Executive was established on 1st September 1969 and the founding directors were:

Director General:
GA (Tony) Harrison (38), the Town Clerk of Bolton, the youngest to hold such a position when appointed aged 33.

Director of Finance and Administration:
DA (David) Graham (41), the Finance Director of Threlfall Chester's Brewery.

Director of Operations & Engineering
GG (Geoff) Harding (45), General Manager of Wallasey Corporation Transport.

Director of Personnel:
E (Ernest) Armstrong who had come from a similar position in Great Universal Stores.

This team combined both experience in the public and private sectors, and each were outstanding in their own right. All the divisional and district jobs were filled from people in the former municipalities, although there were some retirements. Norman Kay was translated from Bury, where he had been the General Manager, to head up the new Southern Division. H (Harry) Taylor, the former General Manager and Engineer of Oldham was translated to become the Divisional Engineer, Central. Peter Bland, the former General Manager and Engineer of Ashton became the Commercial Services Manager responsible for property, private hire and the parcels service previously provided by Manchester and Rochdale. JFW (John) Clarkson joined the Executive team as Financial Controller, having held a similar position in Bolton. DS (Scott) Hellewell joined as Planning Officer from the West Riding County Council, where he had set up their Transportation Planning Section. Previously Scott had thirteen years experience with British Railways. IEM (Ian) Buttress was appointed Secretary; he had previously served in the Town Clerk's Departments in Bolton and Warrington. The Head Office was in Peter House, Oxford Street overlooking St Peter's Square.

The impressive facade leading into Salford's Frederick Road depot, which from 1901 until 1947 had been home to the trams, in addition to the growing bus fleet. Redevelopment has seen wholesale demolition of the site and replacement with modern housing. The frontage is now student accommodation incorporating in its construction the stonework from the arch and the two panels with the date and the coat of arms seen above in this view. Salford's other depot was the more-modern Weaste facility dating from 1929. That has also been redeveloped but the frontage has been retained and incorporated into the new building. A Metro-Cammell bodied ex-Salford Leyland vehicle is about to take up service on the joint route 12 to Bolton. *(JAS)*

This picture: Victoria bus station seen from Greengate with one of LUT's Guy Arabs making the long journey to Liverpool via Atherton. Centre: Victoria Bridge from the top with a selection of Salford vehicles, including the prominently placed Salford Mancunian. Foot: A jumble of cars, buses and a coach in the yard at Frederick Road. The original design as a tram shed is all too obvious and unsuited to good logistical bus operation. *(JAS all)*

The General Managers (sometimes combined with Engineers) of the undertakings were:

Ashton	P Bland	Ramsbottom	J Mort
Bolton	JB Batty	Rochdale	H Procter
Bury	HN Kay	Salford	H Craggs
Leigh	W Mitchell	SHMD	JH Wood
Manchester	J Thompson	Stockport	H Eaton
Oldham	H Taylor		

SELNEC PTE's DIRECTORS & PRINCIPAL OFFICERS

Director General	GA Harrison
Director of Finance & Administration	DA Graham
Director of Operations & Engineering	GG Harding
Director of Industrial Relations	E Armstrong
Secretary	IEM Buttress
Public Relations Officer	RL Smith
Financial Controller	JFW Clarkson
Planning Officer	DS Hellewell
Manager Salaries, Wages & Administration	LJ Trueman
Commercial Manager	P Bland

SELNEC PTE: Divisional Management

Northern Division (Bradshawgate, Bolton)

Associate Director/General Manager	JB Batty
Traffic Manager	H Craggs
Chief Engineer	JG Holden
Personnel Manager	C Burton
Chief Accountant	I Spence

Central Division (Devonshire Street, Manchester)

Associate Director/General Manager	J Thompson
Traffic Manager	J Gillanders
Chief Engineer	H Taylor
Personnel Manager	G Cockayne
Chief Accountant	DC Holley

Southern Division (Daw Bank, Stockport)

Associate Director/General Manager	HN Kay
Traffic Manager	H Eaton
Chief Engineer	B Holcroft
Personnel Manager	JA Morris
Chief Accountant	R Fowles

District Management

Northern Division

Leigh	W Mitchell
Bolton	C Whalley
Bury & Ramsbottom	J Mort
Rochdale	H Reeves

Southern Division

Stockport	F Kennington
Oldham	J Marsh
Ashton/SHMD	JH Wood

Central Division

North West Area Manager	RW Hill
Eastern Area Manager	JA Hall
Southern Area Manager	KE Holt

Whilst one-man-operation was on-going, meaning conductors (or guards) would become redundant, there was still was a shortage of staff for those crew-operated services not yet due for conversion. Thus it was necessary to advertise for conductors whilst also advising the public how to cope with the new arrangements on these vehicles operated only by the driver, whilst also having to get used to the new coinage and values. One-man-operation later became known as one-person-operation (OPO) but at this time bus driving was very largely a male occupation. The advent of power-steering and automatic transmission would make the work more female-friendly. (MMofT all)

SELNEC'S INHERITANCE

The total SELNEC bus fleet on Vesting Day was 2,526 vehicles. There were 2,349 double-deckers of which 465 (20%) were suitable for one-man-operation (omo). There were 177 single-deckers of which 140 (79%) were suitable for omo. There were 817 rear-engined double-deckers in the fleet of which 463 (57%) were suitable for omo. The discrepancy in double-deck omo numbers is accounted for by two PD3s of the Northern Fleet being suitable for omo. This group consisted of 503 Leyland Atlanteans and 314 Daimler Fleetlines. 65% of the double-deck fleet (1,532) were front-engined with rear platforms or forward entrances. Double-deck chassis included AEC Regents and Renowns, Leyland Titan PD2s and PD3s, Daimler CVDs, CVG5s and CVG 6s and a few Guy Arabs and Dennis Lolines. There were 177 single-deckers in the initial SELNEC fleet. There were AEC Reliances with underfloor engines and AEC Swifts with rear-engines and a full range of Leyland underfloor and rear-engined chassis, some Daimler Fleetlines and odd representatives from Albion, Atkinson, Bedford and Bristol.

Naturally, being Lancashire, the most common chassis was a Leyland Titan PD2 or PD3, but some fleets, notably Rochdale and Leigh concentrated on AECs. Rochdale had Regent III and Vs whilst Leigh had AEC Renowns and some Dennis Lolines. Leigh was unusual amongst the municipalities in having an entirely lowbridge double-deck fleet. This occurred because their operating area was criss-crossed by numerous railway and colliery lines all with low bridges. Accordingly the depot was built with a low roof. So in spite of many of the bridges being lifted as the lines closed, the depot still precluded the operation of highbridge buses!

Manchester latterly had a dual-sourcing policy buying both Leylands and Daimlers – its Crossleys were becoming a memory; Salford had standardised on Daimlers for many years but as the need for

(continued on page 23)

One of Ashton's NCME-bodied Atlanteans contrasts with a Guy Arab IV double-decker seen loading behind it at Mossley Hollins School. This particular example has bodywork by Bond of Wythenshawe and was new to Ashton in 1956, remaining in service with SELNEC until 1970. Guys would make a strong comeback when LUT was taken into the fold. (JAS)

Crossley productss had been reasonably well represented throughout the former fleets but no chassis and only 18 bodies passed to **SELNEC**, from Oldham, Ashton and Stockport. Former Stockport 319 serves as reminder of what had gone and carries the distinctive later bodywork, without the raised areas in the rear windows, as it waits below the A6 road just outside the town centre. An example from an earlier batch survives in the Museum collection. *(APY)*

Manchester had a large fleet of Leyland Titan PD2s which passed to SELNEC, many with Metro-Cammell bodywork as here. Number 3679 is standing in a gloomy corner of Stevenson Square, Manchester, about to work on the long-standing 24 route, worked jointly with Rochdale. Manchester had eschewed the larger PD3 models in the face of union demands for better pay for operating larger vehicles with more passengers. The issue finally came to a prolonged head when the larger capacity Atlanteans arrived in 1959. *(STA)*

Three Rochdale vehicles showing the original and later liveries. Number 2, left, is an AEC Reliance, No.42 an AEC Regent III and 267 a Daimler CVG6. All three carry bodywork by Weymann and the difference in body width between the 7ft 6in wide Regent and the 8ft Daimler is clearly seen. With the exception of five Reliances from Salford in the Central Division all the AECs SELNEC inherited pre- NWRC happened to be in fleets in the Northern Division. Joe Franklin, Rochdale's then manager, had been Salford's engineer under Charles Baroth and later moved to take charge at Blackpool. *(APY)*

Bury Corporation buses had a dull light green livery with cream relief as shown in this picture of No. 116, seen in preserved condition, without advertisements, and with the borough crest above the driver's cab between decks – a fashionable position at the time. The Leyland Atlantean has a Liverpool-style Metro-Cammell built body. The front and rear 'peaks' and twin vertical headlamps cannot disguise the generally flat appearance of this vehicle. *(JAS)*

A typical Manchester scene in 1970 with a convoy of ex-MCT buses crossing the junction of Whitworth Street and Oxford Road. The leading bus, 4188 is a Daimler CVG6 with Metro-Cammell bodywork very similar to the Salford vehicle seen on page 11. The bus following is also a Daimler CVG6, but with a 'tin-front' and Burlingham bodywork. The apparent difference in width is caused by the slight taper to the front of the leading vehicle. Note the two different types of MCT destination display: the leading bus has the final destination at the top, the Burlingham at the bottom. Bringing up the rear, an MCT 'Mancunian' in its striking red and white livery also shows the revised positioning. *(DSH)*

5289, a 'tin-front' Leyland Titan PD2 with Roe rear platform body, ex-Oldham Corporation joining Piccadilly from Oldham Street on a service 59 from Shaw (Wrens Nest) to Manchester Piccadilly station. This service was extended to the railway station forecourt in anticipation of the closure of the Manchester-Oldham-Rochdale line – which eventually happened in October 2009 prior to Metrolink conversion *(STA)*

Bolton had a fleet of modern double-deckers including Leyland PD2 and PD3s, Daimler CVG6s and AEC Regent V models, in addition to its distinctive rear-engined Atlanteans. Ralph Bennett had been working towards a more modern design of double-decker, and *en route* had introduced full-fronted vehicles such as this Leyland PD2 with Metro-Cammell bodywork. There were also some rather more attractive examples from ELCB, both makes incorporating forward entrances. The red livery contrasts with the traditional maroon associated with Bolton's buses. *(STA)*

Ashton, Manchester and Stockport vehicles in Ashton's bus station. The Stockport vehicle, far right, will work back to its home town whilst the other two are on former trolleybus workings, the 218 Manchester to Stalybridge and the 127, former 217, Haughton Green service. (JAS)

Reference has been made to the once widespread Parcels Service which Manchester operated from a bespoke facility at Bennett Street, behind the Hyde Road Car Works. The building later became part of the Training School after the parcels operation was moved to the former Parrs Wood depot when that became redundant. The parcels operation suffered a serious financial blow when its main customer, Great Universal Stores (GUS), terminated its contract in the light of more suitable, and competitive, alternatives as the whole international parcels market opened up in 1972. By the mid-1970s the company was becoming just another van hire operation. (MMoT)

replacements for the big post-1951 Daimler intake came, some Leylands reappeared.

After Leyland gave up bodying buses Metro-Cammell became the predominant bodybuilder in the local fleets, although East Lancashire Coachbuilders of Blackburn, and Charles Roe of Leeds, were well represented. Other bodybuilders included: Bond, Burlingham, Longwell Green, Massey Bros, Northern Counties, Alexanders, Crossley, Park Royal, and Weymann. Both Northern Counties and Massey Bros were based in Wigan with the former eventually taking over the latter.

The last outstanding municipal bus order for complete vehicles was delivered in 1972 to SELNEC Central. This was a batch of 34 Daimler Fleetlines (2271-2304) which had been ordered by Manchester. The body order was originally placed with East Lancs but was switched first to Park Royal and then to Roe because of the disruption caused to East Lancs production by the fire at their factory in 1970. These were the only Mancunian type bodies built by Roe. They were also the last Roe bodies to be supplied to the PTE. Mancunians were bodied by Park Royal, Metro-Cammell, Roe and East Lancs. The differences were virtually indiscernable except for the East Lancs examples.

There were, however, still some outstanding chassis orders and these would be used to start the process of developing the SELNEC standard bus as described in a later section.

FLEET RE-NUMBERING SCHEME

1 – 199	Central Division single-deck buses
201 – 299	Coach Fleet
1000 series	Central Division 'Mancunian' Atlanteans
2000 Series	Central Division 'Mancunian' Fleetlines
3000 series	All other Central Division Leyland Buses
4000 series	All other Central Division Daimler Buses
5000 series	Southern Division:
50xx	single-deck buses
51xx – 52xx	ex-Oldham double-deck buses
54xx	ex-Ashton double-deck buses
56xx	ex-SHMD double-deck buses
58xx – 59xx	ex-Stockport double-deck buses
6000 series	Northern Division:
60xx	single-deck buses
61xx x 62xx	ex-Rochdale double-deck buses
63xx	ex-Bury double-deck buses
64xx	ex-Ramsbottom double-deck buses
65xx – 68xx	ex-Bolton double-deck buses
69xx	ex-Leigh double-deck buses

Stockport was one of the fleets which had no double-deck vehicles suitable for one-man-operation when SELNEC was ready to introduce it. The situation was resolved by transferring 13 former Manchester Atlanteans into Daw Bank where they were repainted and made ready for driver-only operation. Number 3819 is seen fresh out of the paint shop and awaiting the fitment of destination blinds for its new area. These vehicles were effectively the replacements for the VRTs lost at ELCB. *(STA)*

THE SELNEC COLOUR SCHEME

One of the early decisions to be made related to the symbol to be adopted and the colour scheme for the fleet. It was the public relations firm of Brunnings (Manchester) who devised both. SELNEC quickly adopted the 'lazy S' symbol with a coloured flash: magenta for the Northern Division, blue for Central and green for Southern. When the Company-organisation was introduced later, the Divisional colours were replaced by the existing SELNEC flash in its *Sunglow Orange*. The white was given the name *Mancunian White*.

The predominant colours of the inherited fleet were red (in many shades) and cream applied in different styles. Exceptions were blue at Leigh, Rochdale and Ashton, light green at Bury, mid-green at SHMD and dark green at Salford, where buses did not carry external advertising for many years. Arguably the best presented fleet was that of Stockport Corporation, also highly standardised on Leyland PD2s and PD3s with East Lancs bodies. Manchester City Transport had pioneered omo of double-deck buses and had introduced the eye-catching and box-like Mancunian body originally sketched by Ken Mortimer, their Public Relations Officer. This was finished in white with two red areas. The remainder of the Manchester Fleet had degenerated to a dull red with a single cream band 'tween decks, similar to London Transport. So what should SELNEC's livery be? A rainbow bus? Orange and off-white was selected and caused a sensation when launched at Hyde Road Garage on 11th March 1970. Emphasis was placed on the safety aspects of the bright colours and the orange in particular.

In March 1970 a fleet renumbering scheme was introduced. It is set out in full on the previous page. In summary ex-Manchester vehicles kept their numbers in the 1 – 4000 series. 5000 was added to buses in the Northern Division and 6000 to buses in the Southern Division. 7000 and upwards was reserved for the forthcoming SELNEC Standards.

Just out of the paint shop and waiting in Daw Bank Garage, Stockport, to be allocated to its garage and take up service is ex-Stockport 'tin front' Leyland PD2 with Crossley bodywork No. 5938, a standard Stockport 27ft 6in x 8ft double-decker. Noteworthy are the drop-down windows at a time when sliding units had long been the norm. This original livery is carried by a former Stockport vehicle in the Boyle Street Museum. Because it was prone to fading the orange was soon replaced with a darker shade, and simultaneously to give a crisper appearance white replaced the cream. The green Southern Division flash can be clearly discerned but fleet numbers are white outlined in gold, ex-Manchester stock. Black Helvetica Light transfers will soon replace them. *(STA)*

The Refuge Assurance building on Oxford Road – now apartments – forms the backdrop to this Mancunian standard showing the new colours. Working the 49 service to Southern Cemetery it was standing outside the BBC building, now due to be relocated to Media City at Salford Quays. Earlier comments about untidy blind displays still apply, frequently beaten only by the dirty patches under fuel caps where spillage was so often not cleaned off. All the money spent on Corporate Image can so easily be wasted in this manner. *(STA)*

Two former **SHMD** Daimler **CVG6s**, both with **NCME** bodywork and seen in Ashton bus station, give a comparison of before and after the new livery had been applied. Originally SHMD number 7 seen above, dating from 1964, has a forward-entrance body and although it carries the new **SELNEC** number – 5607 – the splendid coat of arms can still be seen on the side panel. Below we see No. 5682, newly turned out in **SELNEC** colours and with the Southern Division green flash, ready to depart from the same location on Service 11. The new livery suits its **NCME**-body which in this case has a rear platform. It features the standee-window design, a feature of this bodybuilder and operator. The fuller 'tin-front' (actually grp of course) of this Daimler CVG6 incorporates the headlights and has, arguably, a much more pleasing appearance than the newer vehicle shown above. *(DSH both)*

Stockport sisters side-by-side in their newly opened Daw Bank Garage. Former number 47 now 5847, newly resplendent in SELNEC's sunglow orange, with the green Southern Divisional flash, with number 55, showing off just what a smart fleet the PTE inherited. Both are Leyland Titan PD2s, with East Lancs bodies. To many people's minds, ELCB took over the mantle from Leyland when the chassis builder ceased to build its own bodies. Stockport put off ordering rear-engined vehicles until there was no alternative. They then ordered 10 Bristol VR's, arguably the best of the rear-engined designs, but these were lost through the fire at the Blackburn coachbuilder's factory in 1970 as mentioned elsewhere. *(STA)*

Two more sisters, this time from the Ramsbottom UDC fleet. Number 6409, a PD3 on the right, is still in the municipality's livery, although carrying the SELNEC number. The bus on the left, 6403, is a Leyland PD2 and has been repainted into the new livery and carries the Northern Division magenta flash. It is interesting to note that the older bus carries a later version of Leyland's 'tin' front, but the operator reverted to the classic radiator for later deliveries. Which do you consider more attractive? Otherwise, the buses carry virtually identical East Lancs bodies, but small differences are discernable. Ramsbottom was one of the smallest municipal operators in Lancashire. *(DSH)*

Finance, Fares, Decimalisation & Route Numbers

The first report submitted to the SELNEC PTA on 17th September 1969 showed a revenue requirement of £2,385m, in part because of the anticipated bus deficit of £1.5m and the anticipated funding requirement for the railways of £500,000. Having considered numerous options evaluated by the PTE, it was decided by the PTA not to precept on the rates or to cut services but to obtain the money from fares. For the Central Division services this was to introduce a peak/off-peak differential of 3d (1p). There were also to be different charges on crew and omo routes – both controversial steps at the time.

It should be remembered that in 1969 all the inherited bus operations were overall profitable (except for Manchester) and this policy was to be continued. Fare scales were different between the individual operators taken over, except over common sections of route. This was an unacceptable anomaly for the PTA, who wanted common fare scales throughout the SELNEC area. Not surprisingly Manchester had the highest fares and because of their situation Salford had some of the lowest. This anomaly arose because Salford received its share of the higher fares charged by Manchester and LUT. The first step towards a SELNEC-wide fare scale was for a common farescale for the Northern and Southern Divisions and separate scales for Manchester and Salford within the Central Division. There were two scales: standard and cheap weekday. Over time, fares were brought into line with those appertaining in Manchester until there was a full SELNEC-wide fare scale. Also at this time a conurbation-wide Concessionary Fares Scheme was introduced. In February 1971 decimalisation of the coinage took place and this led to further rationalisation and simplification. Late in 1971 the PTA decided to adopt a rate precept of 3.4p in the pound to allow the PTE to cover the cost of vital social services including concessionary fares, children's fares and unremunerative services. It also covered the £5m deficit on rail services.

Whilst SELNEC had introduced a fleet-wide vehicle numbering scheme in March 1970, the same cannot be said for a network-wide route numbering scheme. There were certain streets where you could see several No. 8s or No. 64s which was acceptable when buses had different liveries, but was totally confusing as the fleets were repainted in the SELNEC colours. This was a major failing by SELNEC, as was the lack of any combined or company timetable books. These were interesting failures of an organisation which was arguably the most progressive of the four original PTEs. Eventually a SELNEC-wide route renumbering scheme was finalised in March1973 and was completed by the time GMPTE was established in 1974. The scheme is shown below.

ROUTE RE-NUMBERING SCHEME

Service 1 – 299	Ex-Manchester & Salford services and ex-NWRC services based on Altrincham, Sale, and Urmston.

This covers GMT's Central area.

Services 300 – 329	Ex-Stockport Corporation
Services 330 – 355	Ex-Ashton Corporation and SHMD
Services 358 – 389	Ex-North Western services based on Stockport.
Services 390 – 399	Ex-North Western Services based on Glossop
Service 400	Trans-Lancs Express
Services 401 – 434	Ex-Oldham Corporation
Services 435 – 467	Ex-Rochdale Corporation
Services 468 – 499	Ex-Bury Corporation and Ramsbottom UDC services
Service 500	Bolton-Airport summer express
Services 501 – 550	Ex-Bolton Corporation
Services 560 – 567	Ex-Bolton Corporation
Services 571 – 582w	Ex-Bolton Corporation
Services 551 – 559	LUT or GMT service based
Services 568 – 570	on Leigh, some of which
Services 583 – 587	were jointly licensed although operated entirely by one operator or the other
Services 588 – 599	Ex-Wigan Corporation
Services 600 – 638	Ex-Wigan corporation
Services 644 – 696	LUT services not based on Leigh.

S. E. Lancashire
—— **N. E. C**heshire
PASSENGER TRANSPORT EXECUTIVE
central division

decimal currency

Passengers are reminded that after midnight on the 31st December, 1969, HALF-CROWNS are no longer legal tender and will not be accepted in payment of fares.

Printed by Warburtons (Printers) Ltd., 35a Old Mill St., Manchester 4. Tel.: COL 4196   1787

FARES REVISION

Commencing SUNDAY, 29th AUGUST, 1971, Revised Fares will be introduced on all services.

Some fare-stages will be amended on certain routes.

Detailed handbills are available from all SELNEC Offices.

SELNEC P.T.E.
Southern Bus Company,
Daw Bank,
Stockport
Tel.: 061-480 4001

H. N. KAY,
Director/General Manager

CONCESSIONARY PASSES for the ELDERLY

Until January 1, 1971, these passes are not available on buses operating in the North Western Road Car Company's area.

Therefore, they cannot be used for the time being on Service Nos. :-

2, 3, 5, 10, 11, 12, 13, 14, 18, 20, 23, 33/34 and 222/223

They are only available between the following points on :-

Service	Available between	Service	Available between
6	Snipe Inn & Hollingworth	108	Piccadilly & Brooklands Road
22	Levenshulme & Longford Pk. Entrance	125	Hyde Bus Station & Hollingworth
44/46	Piccadilly & Altrincham Rd./Park Rd.		

Printed by Warburtons (Printers) Ltd., 35a Old Mill St., Manchester 4. Tel.: COL 4196   2744

Contemporary traffic notices remind us that, in addition to everything else, the new organisation had to cope with the change to decimal currency, and new value coins. Note the style of presentation of the name in the upper example – the lazy S logo has yet to make its appearance. *(MMofT all)*

And now... the <u>facts</u>
about Selnec service

A Report, to the travelling public in the SELNEC area, on public transport in 1970

There is no doubt that SELNEC, your local Passenger Transport Authority and Executive, has been the subject of much uninformed comment—and this Report is therefore presented direct to you so that you may read the facts. Most of them are extracted from the recently-published SELNEC Annual Report and Accounts.

Before setting out these facts, it may be worth reminding you of the structure of SELNEC Passenger Transport Authority. It consists mainly of representatives of all the local authorities in the area; it decides policy and controls the management Executive; and it provides a service on a non-profit-making basis.

The Problems Many problems were inherited by SELNEC. 1970 was the most difficult year that the bus industry has ever experienced, but in this difficult year SELNEC's record—even with the tremendous task of setting up an entirely new organisation—was among the best in the country. Many improvements to the service are still needed, but SELNEC are tackling the problems—vigorously.

Problems on the financial side were extremely difficult, too — particularly when it is realised that the losses of the combined bus authorities (on a comparable basis) were as follows:-
1967/8 loss—£118,000
1968/9 loss—£519,000

The threatened loss for 1970 facing SELNEC at the start was over £3 million! (Taking into account the effects of inflation).

The Action To avoid increasing fares by the full amount needed to offset all this projected loss, SELNEC cut costs, reduced white-collar staff and improved efficiency throughout the organisation. These measures certainly paid off — and helped to limit fare increases. The final result for the calendar year 1970 was a small deficit of £111,000 which could be met from reserves.

During 1970, SELNEC carried out many improvements — and introduced several welcome innovations: They

*Achieved much more reliable bus services in the Northern and Southern Divisions. So much so that loss of service in these areas is now less than one-fifth of that obtaining before SELNEC was formed.

*Tackled problems of basic engineering and bus design—activities that should result in improved reliability in our Central Division by the end of 1971.

*Introduced a concessionary fares system for pensioners, covering the whole area and available on the buses of all operators.

*Introduced the cheap weekday fare period, enabling housewives and pensioners to make long journeys for only a few pence.

*Designed a new, safer and more comfortable standard bus.

*Began the replanning of road/rail passenger transport for the future — developing new approaches to bus services and better rail services.

*Though forced to increase fares during 1970, kept the increase over the last eighteen months down to only half that imposed by comparable operators.

SELNEC are going places
Go places with them—please use <u>your</u> buses.

It soon became apparent that keeping the travelling public informed about just what **SELNEC** was achieving was vital as demonstrated by the item opposite. Clearly there must have been some fairly vociferous criticism to merit such a formal response. A more positive, and certainly well-received approach, was to open the doors and show the world just what happened every day to keep services operating. The 1973 event at the former Hyde Road car works, where many of the buses were repaired and overhauled (and in earlier years the trams had been built), was a tremendous success. Sadly the effects of vandalism could be seen first-hand in buses where the upper deck had been destroyed by fire, as in the upper view, though self-ignition of Atlanteans was by no means unknown. **SELNEC** inherited 26 bus garages and workshops and the lower view, also at Hyde Road, shows a selection of rear-engined double-deckers under repair. On the left is 4704 in **SELNEC** livery next to 4709 still in **MCT** livery. Both are Fleetlines with Metro-Cammell bodywork. The third vehicle is a recently repainted Mancunian, 1164 whilst the ghostly apparition next to it is another Fleetline awaiting application of its orange relief. *(JAS both)*

Visit the **SELNEC** Open Day

Sunday, 17th June, 1973

10-30 a.m. to 4-30 p.m.

THE EXPERIMENTAL VEHICLES

The need for some swift rationalisation of the fleet was obvious when the figures quoted earlier are considered. Ideally all the vehicles should be suitable for one-man-operation, though at this time widespread use of double-deckers in this manner was still some way away – it had, of course, been introduced by Manchester as soon as it became legal in August 1967.

The variety of makes of chassis and bodies was less important than the configuration of the vehicles themselves, for clearly the aim of eliminating conductors could only be achieved with suitable buses. With a mix of vehicle lengths, engine positions, doorway positions, in addition to local agreements allowing for or precluding omo, the whole situation required considerable forward planning.

Such planning might have been much easier had there been suitable vehicles for the task but in SELNEC's eyes there were none. They were not alone in this view but with the number of buses to be replaced the need for standardisation was paramount. It should be remembered that at this time British Leyland had the monopoly and foreign imports were very much in the minority. The three main contenders in the double-deck market were the unreliable Atlantean, the somewhat better Fleetline, and the Bristol VR, of which no examples existed in any of the inherited fleets.

In the single-deck field Leyland was busy phasing out its existing range, including the popular and reliable Bristol RE, to force customers to take the then new and largely unproven Leyland National. The days of choice had gone, and in a situation reminiscent of Henry Ford's "any colour so long as it's black" the National was initially only available in NBC colours — poppy red, leaf green or white. Dark red was added before London would order but no provision was made for the potential business from the PTEs!

SELNEC decided to take 12 Leyland Nationals, but also to take 12 of the new Metro-Scania single-decker which used Swedish running units in a body built by Metro-Cammell in Birmingham, and to compare the performance of the two. Both were very expensive machines, but since single-deckers would form only a small portion of the fleet this was not such a problem. Their unexpected thirst was to prove a greater issue. A further Metro-Scania was added, with its engine encapsulated to reduce noise, and branded the HUSH Bus. The very limited requirement for smaller vehicles — carrying less than 20 passengers — was addressed by working with Oldham manufacturer Seddon.

The Experimental Vehicles

Original No	Renumbered	Registration	Chassis Make & Type	Body Make	Type	Date
EX1-6	5466-5471	PNF941-946J	Leyland Atlantean PDR1 A/1	Northern Counties	H43/32F	1971
EX7-11	6245-6249	TNB747-751K	Daimler Fleetline CRG6LXB	Northern Counties	H43/32F	1972
EX 12-1 6	6395-6399	TNB752-756K	Daimler Fleetline CRG6LXB	Northern Counties	H43/32F	1972
EX17-21	6250-6254	TNB757-761K	Daimler Fleetline CRG6LXB	Northern Counties	H45/27D	1972
EX22-29 not used						
EX30-37	1330-1337	TXJ507-514K	Leyland National 1151/2R		B46D	1972
EX38-41	1338-1341	VVM601-604L	Leyland National 1051/2R		B40D	1973
EX42-49`	1342-1349	TXJ515-522K	Metro-Scania BR111MH		B44D	1972
EX50-53	1350-1353	VVM605-608L	Metro-Scania BR110MH		B40D	1973
EX54-55	1354-1355	WVM668-669L	Mercedes-Benz O.305	Northern Counties	B43D	1973
EX56-58	1700-1702	YDB453-455L	Seddon Pennine IV:236	Seddon	DP25F	1972
EX59	6059	XBN976L	Seddon Pennine IV:236	Seddon	DP25F	1972
EX60	1360	VVM609L	Metro-ScaniaBR110		B40D	1973
EX61	1361	XVU387M	Seddon-Chloride	Seddon	B43D	1973
EX62	1362	GNC276N	Seddon-Lucas	Seddon	B19F	1975
EX100		CWO600K	Levland-Crompton	Willowbrook	B19F	1972

EX1-6 had chassis ordered by Ashton and were the first prototypes of Selnec's standard double-decker.
EX7-11,17-21 had chassis ordered by Rochdale.
EX12-16 had chassis ordered by Bury.
EX30 was the first production Leyland National.

EX59 was subsequently renumbered 1703.
EX60 had an encapsulated engine and was marketed as the Hush Bus.
EX61 was delivered as XVU87M. It was promoted as the Silent Rider.
EX100 was on loan from the Department of Trade & Industry during 1973.
EX61 and EX62 did not carry their new numbers 1361/2.

The immediate point of recognition on the Metro-Scania vehicles, seen opposite, single and later double-deck, was the asymetrical windscreen which gave the driver better kerbside vision and the bus a lop-sided look. EX45 is one of eight 11-metre 44-seat examples and is working the 66 Circular service in Bolton, to Great Lever. A small card in the windscreen announces **EXACT FARE ONLY** , meaning no change will be given, but there is no mention that no conductor is carried. There were also four of the shorter – 10-metre – 40-seaters. *(STA)*

There were also eight 11-metre and four 10-metre Leyland Nationals, the two-door arrangement being again adopted though the longer version seated two more than the Metro-Scanias. Northern Counties fitted the standard SELNEC driver's interior cab door with its ticket-issuing equipment and change tray and applied the orange relief and transfers since Leyland's one-bus-suits-all approach did not cater for such items. Small wonder that selling Leyland Nationals would be hard work outside the captive NBC market. EX35 is working the same 66 service for direct comparison. *(STA)*

EX30, the first production Leyland National from the new purpose-built Workington facility, seen here splendidly restored outside the Museum of Transport, illustrates the dual-door arrangement, and also the air-conditioning pod at the rear of the roof. A later model, without this pod, was later made available to help reduce the cost and complexity of the vehicle. Note the slip board, not announcing *No Conductor*, but instead *Temporary Conductor* when circumstances dictated such measures. The National firmly established in passenger's minds that the days of comfortable seats had, like the presence of conductors, become a thing of the past. The various EX vehicles apparently created problems with the maintenance staff, doubtless over allowance of time and bonus pay issues for working on 'oddballs', in amongst the additional work in monitoring their on-the-road performance. Life in the transition period was rarely boring. *(JAS)*

Four Seddon Pennine IV models were purchased in 1972. These 19-seat vehicles were bodied by Seddon's subsidiary Pennine Coachcraft. EX56 is seen here on the Stockport bus park between duties on the 376 Hazel Grove Circular. Thirty-nine further Seddons were purchased, with a revised body style, and differing seating arrangements, and then a final fortieth example which was battery-powered. The type found its way onto the city centre shoppers' service in Manchester, being ideally suited to the narrow streets in the King Street area. Their success led to what has today become the three free bus services in Manchester, with other towns following suit. *(JAS)*

The main effort, in terms of design time and long-term planning, would clearly have to be invested in a double-decker which could operate throughout the whole of the SELNEC area, and be capable, when the time came, of operation by driver only. The magnitude, and success, of this project merits a section to itself (page 38) but at this stage the way was open to begin to address the requirements.

Inevitably, there were outstanding orders from the constituents when SELNEC came into being and since these included 6 Atlantean and 15 Fleetline chassis these formed the guinea pigs for the embryo Standard double-decker, with Northern Counties of Wigan being chosen as the bodybuilder. Local suppliers were considered important although at that stage NCME had nowhere near the capacity to build what would be required in terms of volume.

The full story of the experimental buses would fill a volume on its own but from these trials came the eventual decisions to purchase what became the

EX1 photographed by the author when new and posed at the back of Hyde Road garage in the former tramcar permanent way yard. The first six experimental vehicles were based on Atlantean chassis which had been ordered by Ashton. It was considered appropriate to allocate them to Ashton, or more correctly SELNEC Southern, when they became numbers 5466-5471, not least because they were non-standard in many respects once the final specification had been drawn up. Matters such as cab switching locations for lighting and door controls, for instance, varied from bus to bus and were more safely handled in a small fleet with less drivers in the rosters. Flat windscreens were originally incorporated but caused a build up of dirt around the front and first bays of the lower deck due to the slipstream, causing mirrors to be rendered useless without frequent cleaning. Note that the route number blind is still positioned on the offside, one of the many changes made before production examples went into build. (DSH)

fleet-standard vehicles — and the realisation that some were to prove less successful than others.

Amongst **SELNEC's** many achievements was the work it carried out with manufacturers on the development of battery-powered vehicles. A Seddon midibus, using Lucas electrics, worked on the Centreline service for some time. This led to the decision to use a full-size Seddon chassis and Seddon body for the **SELNEC** Silent Rider. This was powered by Chloride batteries, whose factory was at Clifton Junction. The chassis needed strengthening to carry the extra load and the complete ensemble weighed in at over 12tons 17cwt. It was not a success, and spent much of its time out of service, though it did attain some fame by being displayed at an electric vehicle exhibition in Chicago in 1977. *(DSH both)*

Shown here is one of the production batch of the diesel-powered midis developed from the smaller units and now preserved at Boyle Street. The cost of riding what had by then become the **CENTRELINE** service had risen to 12p. Their successors today offer free travel in the City Centre. *(JAS)*

Two views of **EX54** the prototype semi-integral Mercedes-Benz with Northern Counties two-door single-deck bodywork. This was the British equivalent of the VoV standard bus built by different German chassis and body manufacturers. It had some similar styling characteristics having large, deep windows, flat windscreens, pantograph wipers and a square roofline. Its rear-mounted engine permitted a low floor line for two-thirds of its length. **SELNEC** encouraged the co-operation of Mercedes and **NCME** as a competitor to the Leyland National and Metro-Scania and Ron Parsons, the Wigan company's chief designer, spent some time at the German Mercedes plant with Harry Taylor before work began. The finished result is seen here in Hyde Road garage before entering service in 1973. Despite all this effort only these two vehicles were produced; originally allocated to LUT and then transferred to Oldham they gave some nine year's service. *(DSH both)*

WANTED – A BETTER DOUBLE-DECKER

Leyland Atlantean AN68

SELNEC was the leading PTE in working with Leyland in the re-engineering of the Atlantean rear-engined double-decker. Leyland had pioneered the introduction of such vehicles in 1956, with the first production model being displayed at the 1958 Commercial Motor Show. The first Atlantean into service was operated by Wallasey Corporation where Geoff Harding was the General Manager and who had now become a Director at SELNEC. Reliability of the original design was poor, so much so that spare ratios for Atlanteans were 20-25%, as compared with 10% or less with PD3 or similar front-engined chassis. Whilst this might have been tolerable when the majority of the fleet was front-engined, it became unsustainable when the proportion of rear-engined buses represented 35% of the fleet. Daimler (still a separate company) had learnt from Leyland's mistakes and had produced the Fleetline which was potentially a far superior vehicle.

SELNEC Standard double-decker

In parallel with the AN68 developments, Harry Taylor, who by now had been appointed Chief Development Engineer, was keen to produce a bus body that would suit the operating conditions of the whole of the SELNEC area. Ashton Corporation had an order for Atlantean chassis and it was decided to use these as the basis for the new SELNEC Standard double-decker. Northern Counties Motor and Engineering Co. Ltd. (NCME) of Wigan were selected to design and build the six prototypes EX1 – EX6. The initial order was for six single-door double-deckers seating 75 with a standing allowance for 20. EX1 was exhibited at the 1970 Commercial Motor Show and caused a considerable stir. They were tried out in each of the Districts with passenger and crew reactions being collated. A further 15 prototypes, five with a two door arrangement, as was customary at the time for omo, were ordered for mid-1971 delivery. They featured a rearward-ascending staircase and had a seating capacity of 72 with a standing allowance for 20. After extensive testing and development work the first order was placed with NCME in 1971. By the time GMPTE had ceased to be a bus operator, in October 1986, some 1725 SELNEC Standard buses had been produced on both Leyland and Daimler chassis (in addition to the 21 experimental examples). Most were built by NCME but Park Royal built one fifth. When Lancashire United Transport (LUT) became part of GMPTE they, too, took

SELNEC Standards on Fleetline chassis. They had, of course, already been operating long-wheelbase Fleetlines with NCME bodies similar to the Standard outline, but interestingly these had 'filled-in' backs. NCME had also bodied the two Mercedes Benz 0.305 semi-chassis mentioned earlier. Two virtually

standard bodies were built on Foden chassis for GMT in 1976, when NCME became concerned that its finanical viability as a bodybuilder was in jeopardy whilst Leyland was developing semi-integral models for bodying in its own factories, potentially cutting out NCME and also Alexanders who were simliarly worried.

At this stage mention should be made of two non-SELNEC characters who had a major influence on the development of the SELNEC Standard bus: HG (Henry) Lewis Jnr, and D (David) Cherry. Henry Lewis was the Chairman of NCME and, coincidently, a Director of LUT. David Cherry was the Managing Director of NCME and, came from a 'bus family'. His father, George, had been Manager at Rochdale and later Birkenhead and son David was an outstanding bus engineer who came to Wigan from the National Bus Company. The speedy and successful development of the SELNEC Standard bus, and the steady completion of the large on-going orders, would have been difficult without the determination and dedication of these two people.

Facing page: This picture sums up what a quantum leap forward the Mancunian design was when compared to the Metro-Cammell standard product. Ken Mortimer later revealed that Park Royal were not overjoyed at having to work to his outline design. (JAS)

The first production standard, Atlantean 7001, arrived from Park Royal in 1972. The difference in appearance can be seen when comparing this view with those of the NCME product overleaf. The SELNEC Standard vehicles were designed around a 9.5m chassis which was considered preferable operationally to the 10.5m chassis used on the Manchester Mancunians and also for LUT's Jumbo Daimler Fleetlines with bodies similar in outward appearance to the new Standards, see page 67. (JAS)

The first of the new design of double-deckers were based on Atlantean chassis outstanding from an order placed by Ashton and caused quite a stir at the 1970 Commercial Motor Show at Earls Court in London. These views show EX1 posed on the Hyde Road garage park, when brand-new. All six had single-door NCME bodywork though there were detail differences between them. The views show to perfection the stylish integration of body design and livery and the attention to detail that was put into these vehicles. Subsequently EX 1-6 were numbered 5466-71 and placed into the Ashton-based fleet. None of the Standards carried chassis maker's badges on the front until the arrival of the two Fodens, that distinction being the outcome of some gentle encouragement by this publisher at a meeting with David Cherry and Ron Parsons of Northern Counties at the Wigan premises of the bodybuilder. *(DSH both)*

The 15 Daimler Fleetlines were outstanding from an order placed by Rochdale, becoming EX7-11 and 17-21, and Bury, EX12-16. The final five were fitted with dual-doorway bodywork and the difference is immediately apparent on the offside by the location of the windows in these two views when compared to the single-door version on the opposite page. They became numbers 6245-49, 6250-54 and 6395-99 when allocated into the main fleet. EX17, *aka* 6250 is seen here in Hyde. Note that by now the route number position has moved to the nearside, making it easier to see from a distance when vehicles were bunched in a line in traffic approaching a bus stop. The rear opening window on the upper-deck of the earlier design seen opposite on the Atlantean has been dispensed with, and the staircase has been moved towards the rear, but otherwise the body designs are almost identical. *(STA both)*

Two further views showing the outward differnces between the two manfacturer's products, with the Park Royal-bodied Atlantean example in the Southern fleet being seen in Stockport. The NCME example, below, on a Fleetline chassis, shows the minimal change to livery when GMPTE took over the fleet. Having sorted out its body requirements, and secured a great improvement in the design and reliability of the revised Atlantean, the AN68, the new generation Manchester area buses seemed set to dominate the scene for some time to come. Indeed they did, but problems at suppliers and manufacturers during and after the infamous three-day working week when electricity supplies were insufficient to meet the country's needs, caused considerable slippage. At the time GMT took over the price of the vehicles was around £17,000 for an Atlantean, and £18,000 for a Fleetline with the more expensive Gardner engine. *(JAS both)*

THE COLOURFUL CHANGEOVER PERIOD

Although it took some time for the routes to be renumbered, with the 92 now having become the 192, it took even longer to repaint all the vehicles into their new colours, and some were withdrawn without ever being repainted. This shot was taken in GMT days and the registration of the white car confirms that it is a post-1976 view. Two Mancunians can be seen, the one in the background has been repainted into orange and white whilst 2194 was delivered in the new livery – meanwhile the former Manchester Daimler 4603 soldiers on in its original colours. Just visible is one of Ashton's Roe-bodied Leylands working the extended 66 service described more fully on the next page. In the background the long-standing Lewis's lettering reminds many thousands of shoppers where to go for so many of their requirements – doubtless many will visit the bargain basement. Just out of sight to the right are the steps to 55 Piccadilly, former headquarters of Manchester City Transport and its Managers. The famous clock will by now be permanently showing 12 midnight, the witching hour. *(STA)*

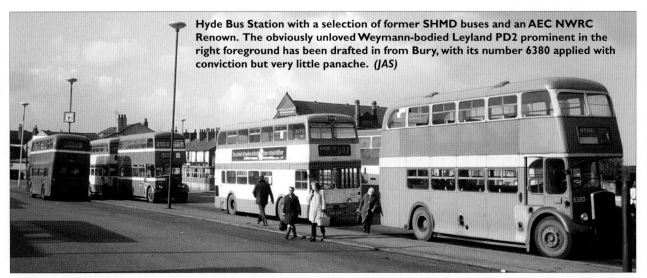

Hyde Bus Station with a selection of former SHMD buses and an AEC NWRC Renown. The obviously unloved Weymann-bodied Leyland PD2 prominent in the right foreground has been drafted in from Bury, with its number 6380 applied with conviction but very little panache. *(JAS)*

Patience would frequently be rewarded with two or three operators in the frame, five was somewhat of a bonus, as in this 1971 view. The North Western Renown is behind a Salford Atlantean, itself waiting at the lights behind a Stockport PD3. The Ashton PD2 awaits its turn and frames the newly repainted SHMD Bristol RE single-decker. *(JAS)*

Scenes like this one in Old Glossop, terminus of the jointly-operated 125 route from Manchester, were numbered when this photograph was taken in 1971 for with the removal of conductors by omo, reversing without a look-out would be stopped. Turning circles sprang up through the country as operators and planning authorities addressed the situation. This ex-Manchester PD2, Metro-Cammell-bodied number 3698, is a mere stone's throw away from the former local tram terminus at the Queens Arms in Old Glossop. The bus terminus was later extended some hundred yards or so to a suitable riverside circle. *(JAS)*

Facing page centre: Ashton bus station in 1971 showing a former Salford Atlantean working the revised 64 service to Peel Green via Eccles and Patricroft. Originally terminating on Victoria Bridge, Manchester, it has now been extended to Ashton (as also was the 66 which operated through Monton first) by combining it with the former 219 service. A former Stockport Titan PD2 waits departure in the background as does a former Oldham Atlantean with Roe bodywork and now in SELNEC colours. *(JAS)*

Stockport's Mersey Square had been an important terminus since the early days of the trams. The Corporation's trolleybuses began running through here from their depot and then from St Peter's Square to Offerton in 1913, and motor buses made their appearance around 1920. Further interest was added in 1921 with the arrival of BRITISH buses, the forerunner of the giant North Western Road Car Company, later also based in Stockport, at Charles Street, where its offices, garage and works were situated. In this view a former Corporation Leyland PD2 with rare Longwell Green bodywork leaves on the 317 service, carrying the white patch with green SELNEC flash for the southern division. Other vehicles in the picture include a former North Western Marshall-bodied standard BET single-decker and two of SELNEC's Stockport allocation of Bristol VRs with Eastern Coach Works bodies with one of Stockport's East Lancashire-bodied Titans. Pickford's removals warehouse stands next to the Mecca bingo hall, the previously well-known Plaza cinema. The single storey building in the right foreground is the North Western traffic office, whilst buses being moved to that company's parking lot would pass under the A6 – out of view to the right – to gain access. Under all this activity the culverted river Mersey goes quietly about its business. *(JAS)*

Glossop's Norfolk Arms Hotel had long been the terminus of the jointly operated – Manchester, North Western, SHMD and Ashton – service but here we see a former Stockport vehicle, now with **SELNEC** Southern, operating the number 6 route to Lower Mosley Street. One of North Western's Glossop-based Renowns, sporting **SELNEC** Cheshire markings, is working the alternative 125 service and heading for Old Glossop from Piccadilly. The white Rover 3500 car was a popular choice at the time. *(JAS)*

Behind the wall above the river Irwell those tall enough could see this panorama of the former Salford Victoria bus station, with its selection of operators. Manchester were late comers but **LUT** and Bolton, operating the joint service number 8 with Salford, were long-standing users. The handsome Bennett Atlantean in the foreground will not be improved by its forthcoming new livery. Manchester Exchange railway station stands behind the inbound ex-Salford **PD2** whilst, in days of yore, Thomas Cook had an office where the photographer stood in 1971 for bookings on the-then river boats. A Salford Mancunian stands alongside a **PD2** at the foot of Victoria Bridge's loading point whilst the infamous Greengate Arches are just out of sight to the right of the picture. Leigh vehicles added to the variety from there, working the jointly-operated **LUT**-Salford-Leigh 26 service back to their home town. The dark green bus shelter was made from saloon doors from withdrawn trams and many still carried their etched coat of arms until the entire edifice was demolished. Waste-not-want-not. *(JAS)*

Glossop was the eastern-most outpost of the **SELNEC** empire. The Norfolk Arms Hotel had been the North Western terminus since their services took over from the Glossop trams in 1927 and the former Stockport Leyland PD2, now in **SELNEC** colours, is ready to return to Manchester on the joint number 6 route. The as-yet unrepainted SHMD Daimler is about to climb the hill *en route* to Hadfield whilst a former North Western single-decker in Henry Street carries the difficult to see **SELNEC** Cheshire brown logo on its red paint scheme. Glossop railway station, with its electrified service to Manchester Piccadilly, is behind the single-decker. *(JAS)*

We have seen the large white rectangle on a Stockport vehicle on page 45, here one of SHMD's rather stylish **NCME**-bodied Titans has been similarly treated. An example of a total repaint of a transferred Stockport Leyland into SHMD green at this time suggested an air of dis-satisfaction with matters within the paint shop *(JAS)*

Rochdale Bus Station bus park containing a selection of former Rochdale Corporation and Yelloway vehicles. Two AEC Regent V's with attractive Weymann bodies, one repainted in **SELNEC** livery, stand with a Metro-Cammell bodied-Daimler Fleetline with the final Rochdale livery. The Weymann AEC Reliance single-decker in the new colours completes the **SELNEC** ensemble whilst the three Yelloway Reliances give a reminder of just how smart that fleet was in its heyday. *(APY)*

One of SHMD's Daimler Fleetlines, renumbered as 5635 but still carrying its SHMD
crest, seen in glorious detail right, stands in Hyde bus station alongside another Northern
Counties-bodied vehicle from the same fleet, recognisable by the standee windows fitted
in the lower deck. (JAS)

Stalybridge bus station was another good spot to see the various liveries of the former
municipalities – while they lasted. This 1971 view shows former SHMD Daimler Fleetline
41, now SELNEC Southern 5641, with Ashton, Manchester and transferred Stockport
vehicles in the distance. This was formerly also the terminus of the trolleybus route from
Piccadilly, jointly operated by Manchester and Ashton vehicles. (JAS)

Ashton had 17 Atlanteans and the photographer managed to catch three together in this view, with 5462 leading and working the Hurst Circular. Note that its **NCME** body has two doors whilst the similarly-shaped Roe body behind on number 51 has only one. The eight Roe-bodied buses had been purchased as trolleybus replacements. By the time the last four **NCME** examples arrived **SELNEC** had been formed and they arrived in its Southern livery. The in-house advertisement for vehicle hire, from a small coach through to a double-decker, was a well-used and eye-catching poster instantly recognisable throughout the area. *(STA)*

Bolton had been amongst the operators determined to avoid the rear-engined models whilst more reliable alternatives were still available. By this time British Leyland had established a monopoly and was gradually phasing out the much preferred and more dependable models to keep up production levels of the Atlantean, Bristol VR and Leyland National. Even the hugely popular and, at this time, much more reliable Fleetline was under threat. Bolton's Leyland PD3 with its unusual full-fronted Metro-Cammell bodywork is seen in Bury with a local Atlantean and a Rochdale Fleetline, the latter newly repainted in corporate livery, about to pass on the 21 service. *(JAS)*

The **SELNEC** Stand at the 'Transpo 73' Exhibition in Salford Docks. The 'caravan', which provided the centre-piece, was built especially by **NCME** for these occasions and was often used to display the Picc-Vic scheme. Unfortunately, it was un-powered and had to be taken to sites on a low-loader. It was, nevertheless, well used. *(APY)*

In many ways a more practical solution, certainly for outside displays, was this Exhibition & Support Vehicle, based on a NCME-built 2-door Standard double-decker, 7232, with a Daimler Fleetline chassis. Seen here in preservation outside the Manchester Museum of Transport in Boyle Street it forms part of the **SELNEC** Preservation Society's large fleet and acts as a support vehicle at rallies. The selection of transfers it carries will be noticed as also will the plug-in power feed from a land line in the Museum. *(JAS)*

As originally established the PTE's had extensive powers to undertake virtually anything related to transport. **SELNEC** used these to the full, acquiring a number of coach operators, expanding the parcel service and, as shown here, setting up Travel Offices. This one was at Piccadilly. *(APY)*

Nevertheless, **SELNEC** kept its eye on the basics – it had some 12,000 bus stops in its area. This stop post in St. Peters Square shows the **SELNEC** version of the National bus stop sign. This is typical of many signs, particularly in Central Manchester. **MCT** had a policy of connecting all points of the compass with the City Centre. Arguably this led to an over-complicated network for both passenger and operator. *(APY)*

An essential piece of equipment is the Service Van. This shows a Central Division Ford Escort van passing through Piccadilly *en route* to its next call. The Engineer's Department vans included a good range of equipment for light running repairs. Other vans were used by the Traffic or Publicity Sections. The location is very close to 55 Piccadilly, which was, for many years, the Head Office of MCT before they moved to their purpose-built office at 2 Devonshire Street North, Ardwick, which was adjacent to Hyde Road garage. Many assumed that Devonshire Street would become the Head Office of SELNEC, but the Directors thought differently and took accommodation in Peter House in Central Manchester. The buses in the background are a Standard on the 113x for Sale, double-banking a **SELNEC** Cheshire Fleetline/Alexander in all-over Quicks advertising livery bound for Middleton and with a Burlingham-bodied Leyland Titan PD2 on its stand bound for Waterhead on the 82 service. The low height of the former North Western vehicle, common to all its double-deckers is clearly apparent. *(STA)*

A long-time favourite – SELNEC's Open Top bus, 5995, had been the former Stockport Corporation's 295 , a Leyland PD2 with cut-down Leyland double-deck body. It was new in 1951. On this occasion it is carrying a Pipe Band advertising a GM Open Day. Black numerals and legal lettering are now evident. Following closely is a Leyland Tiger PS1 with Alexander's body from the Bluebird fleet by then in preservation and housed at Boyle Street. *(APY)*

ALL-OVER ADVERTISING LIVERIES

If **SELNEC** livery was less than popular with some undertakings the application of all-over advertising must have been received with horror. Salford, which had not carried advertising on its green buses, might have been one such example. This cleverly presented ex-North Western Fleetline evidently caused some angry protests from some passengers when they realised that from the outside they appeared through the windows as though they were seated on racing greyhounds. *(JAS)*

A Daimler Fleetline Mancunian, 2274, advertising the *Manchester Evening News* with is snappy slogan 'A friend dropping in'. A somewhat garish, but eye-catching scheme, with which the orange wheels clash. The *MEN* was the largest selling evening paper outside London, and part of the Guardian Group. It was pro-PTE, was and still is pro-public transport. Behind is the somewhat more discreet Yellow Pages bus, *avant garde* in its use of mirror image lettering so that motorists could read its message in their mirrors. Both vehicles, with the Bell Vue Greyhound Fleetline, were on display at the successful Hyde Road Open Day in 1973. *(JAS)*

The first Standard to receive all-over advertising was dual-door EX20 (later 6253), approaching Rochdale Road depot in its striking BarclayCard scheme. *(JAS)*

The secret of success, as ever, was keep it simple. Over complicated and so-called clever schemes could pass by without time for them to register – rather like the lower case lettering on indicator blinds which was introduced as a fashion fad. Not all new ideas would be based on good old common sense. *(JAS)*

SELNEC COACH OPERATIONS

Trans-Lancs Express

In February 1970 the Trans-Lancs Express service, linking Stockport with Bolton round the east and north sides of Manchester, was launched. Route 400, as it was numbered, ran in addition to the various existing routes linking Stockport-Ashton-Oldham-Rochdale-Bury and Bolton. It was operated on a Limited Stop basis, initially by Bedford VAL coaches with 52-seat Plaxton bodywork. As traffic grew new MCW Metropolitan double-deckers were introduced. These were striking looking and fast machines, but were expensive at c£21,000, and thirsty, on at least one occasion a bus ran out of fuel! With a capacity of only c50 gallons, 2-speed gearbox and consumption under 5mpg, they were unable to meet their daily schedule and needed frequent filling up. At one stage it seemed as though bus 'flight-refuelling' might be needed!

At the time the Trans-Lancs Express service was launched there existed a parallel train service between Oldham and Rochdale carrying on to Bury (Bolton Street) and Bolton. This offered a basically hourly service with peak-period augmentation. It received about £380,000 in grant. The railway scene is dealt with later in the book but in this context SELNEC PTE allowed the closure of the Rochdale-Bury(Bolton Street)-Bolton section with the new express bus service providing a reasonable alternative replacement.

TRANS-LANCS EXPRESS Coach service

Stockport to Bolton

Fast, thirsty, expensive and short-lived – the Metropolitans were withdrawn when their first C of F expired. (JAS)

Top: OND739H, No. 222, seen here in Mersey Square working the Trans-Lancs Express, was one of eight Seddon Pennine IV models purchased in 1970 and fitted with Plaxton bodywork. A further eight were purchased the following year. (JAS)

Above: Working the return journey out of Mersey Square and heading for Bolton is number 60, an ECW-bodied Leopard new in 1973. (JAS)

Right: TNB441K seen leaving Piccadilly and entering Market Street heading for Victoria Station was the last of six Duple-bodied Bedford YRQ models purchased in 1972. (STA)

Hale Barns Express

Another innovation, launched on 20th April 1970, was the Hale Barns Executive Coach service linking Hale Barns – an executive-style development south of Altrincham – to Manchester City Centre. This offered luxury coach travel for the commuter with tea, coffee and newspapers being served by a hostess. It was a pioneering attempt to serve the executive commuter market and to tempt motorists to leave their car at home. Whilst a reasonable success, the experiment was not tried elsewhere because of non-competitive journey times. Indeed there were those who said that a well-designed feeder bus service and a through-ticket to the train at Altrincham station should have been developed, but at the time BR were unsympathetic and the train service was not sufficiently attractive.

Below: The coaching operations were eventually branded as Charterplan. This Duple Dominant-bodied Leopard, No. 68, was the last of a batch of three purchased in 1973. (STA)

Printed by Warburtons (Printers) Ltd.,

Centreline
12p fare No change

The Centreline service was introduced in July 1974 with an attractive fare of just 2p to provide a direct and frequent bus service between the railway station forecourts at Piccadilly and Victoria – a precursor to the then proposed Picc-Vic Tunnel. By the time the above view was taken the fare had risen to 5p. Centreline was operated by the later version of Seddon Pennine midis which incorporated considerably deeper windows giving passengers a much better view, useful in the narrow streets when looking for a landmark stop – two are shown here, 1732 followed by 1729, passing Piccadilly Gardens *en route* from Victoria. The service proved very popular and, in later years, other central area distributor services were started. *(STA)*

Slip Boards were attached to the front and sides of the Centreline buses, in part to differentiate the service, and in part to highlight the 'No change' policy which quite soon crept up to a 12p fare due to inflation. The in-house advertising would be seen by many thousands of motorists and taxi drivers stuck behind the well-patronised buses as they weaved their way around the city centre. Whether the message was appreciated or just further aggravation has to be a matter of judgement! *(JAS)*

Standardisation came at a price of course; the loss of the old and much-loved liveries was a blow. Whether in Rochdale, top and centre, or Bury, lower, the colours were always the same.

In this quiet scene in Rochdale two of the fleet's AECs can be seen, the Swift with its Pennine body and in the distance the handsome Regent V with Weymann bodywork.

Although the Rochdale Fleetline, centre, is clean and smart, it can hardly be described as handsome in the manner of the earlier Weymann bodies.

Alexanders made a better job of designing a body for the rear engined chassis and this Bury example on a Daimler Fleetline shows the improvement obtained by shaped front glasses. North Western took the low height version of this body. (JAS all)

Top: A former Manchester Titan with Metro-Cammell bodywork waits outside Littlewood's store in Piccadilly before leaving for Waterhead. The MCTD distinctive bus stop can be seen on the bus shelter.

Centre: One of Salford's rather ungainly double-door Park Royal-bodied Fleetlines in the erstwhile Victoria Bus Station.

Foot: Almost straight out of the paint shops this former SHMD Fleetline with NCME bodywork was seen at the former trolleybus turning loop terminus at Gee Cross, Hyde. See also rear cover illustration.

Sharp eyed readers will note that out of six vehicles shown on these two pages the four equipped for omo all carry different signage. Standardisation? *(JAS all)*

NORTH WESTERN

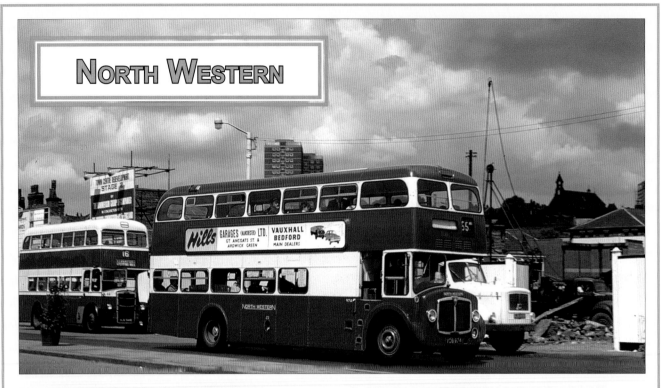

T he North Western Road Car Company was orininally based in King Edward Street, Macclesfield, but moved into Stockport in 1924. Its office was originally in Mersey Square, but a purpose-built Head Office and depot and engineering complex was soon created in Charles Street. It became the overhaul and heavy repair centre for the fleet which at maximum reached c600, buses, coaches and dual-purpose vehicles. With the freedom of action given to BET companies it was largely free to follow its own choice in selection of vehicle makes, within the confines of 'approved' models where satisfactory purchase and warranty arrangements existed of course, in addition to proven reliability.

It operated a very profitable concern, running local buses in Manchester, Lancashire, Yorkshire, Cheshire, Derbyshire and Staffordshire in addition to trunk express routes to Blackpool and London, amongst many others. Coach operation and private hire also kept many of its vehicles busy.

An AEC Renown with low-height Park Royal double-deck forward-entrance body running on the 55, having just overtaken one of Stockport's many PD2s. NWRC had 33 of these AECs. The major development in the background marks the beginning of the giant Merseyway Shopping Centre. Latterly North Western had just four classes of double-decker, Renowns, Alexander-bodied low-height Fleetlines and Dennis Lolines of two types. Foot of the page: North Western finally gained some genuine highbridge buses around 1970 when these Metro-Cammell-bodied Leyland Titans from Ribble including HRN 38 and HCK464, nearest the camera, arrived at Charles Street – to join the driver training fleet! Two are seen here, together with one of NWRC's Dennis Lolines and the preserved ex-Stockport Crossley double-decker, parked here in the yard at the back out of harm's way. They later gained orange and white livery, passed to GMT, and survived until c1980. *(STA both)*

When the core bus business was taken into SELNEC its remaining fleet was divided between Trent, Crosville, and the newly formed coach operation branded as National Travel (North West) Ltd.

Dennis Lolines provided an answer to the low height problem and 15 joined the fleet in 1960 and 1961, all passing to SELNEC. These first examples of the NWRC Loline model were bodied by East Lancashire Coachbuilders but the final 34, numbers 872-895 of which 880 is shown in Mersey Square, were Loline IIIs and carried Alexander bodywork. Some of these Lolines passed to Crosville with Renowns and Fleetlines on the split-up. (RGR)

North Western's Manchester garage was situated at Hulme Hall Road in Cornbrook, Manchester, alongside the railway line to Altrincham, and making use of space under the railway arches within the depot complex. A large open area in front of the garage formed an ideal parking ground and provided opportunities for photography. Number 414, JMA414L, was the second of a batch of five Bristol REs with ECW coach bodywork. It did not pass to SELNEC but became part of the successor coach operation mentioned in the text. Behind it is a Leyland Leopard with a classic Alexander 'Y' type body as illustrated on page 65. (JAS)

Number 321 a Bristol RE with Alexander 'Y' type body still in North Western colours, but with the fleet name deleted and the SELNEC Cheshire transfer beneath the cab. In a smart livery and with coach seats the attractive 'Y' type was an excellent coach and became a classic in bodywork design. The A6 trunk road runs above and behind the bus park here. (STA)

SAVINGS

One of the reasons for setting up the PTEs in the major conurbations was the scope for rationalisation of routes, services and garages/ workshops that came as a by-product of integrating the various separate bus operators. Comment has already been made about subsuming Ramsbottom into Bury and combining SHMD and Ashton into Tameside. Rochdale Road garage in Manchester, opened in 1938 to house the new trolleybus fleet serving the routes east of the City, was closed. Parrs Wood garage at East Didsbury, an excellent site for a bus/train interchange on the Styal line was closed, but used as a base for SELNEC Parcels and ultimately sold to a supermarket group. Stockport had built a new workshop and garage at Daw Bank which permitted the vacation of the unsanitary premises in Heaton Lane and Mersey Square. In an interview with the Sunday Times in November 1971, Geoff Harding was able to claim that in the two years since the establishment of SELNEC, 650 staff had been saved; 170 buses had been taken out of the fleet and two garages, referred to above, had been closed, although there were still 20 remaining. There had been a £1m saving in operating costs. Later a new garage was built in Tameside to house the combined fleets and Bolton's four garages were rationalised into one, Bridgman Street, which was rebuilt. Several garages were modernised, including Bury.

RE-ORGANISATION

It will come as little or no surprise that running a bus operation the size of SELNEC was a very demanding and time-consuming business, even with the pyramidical structure set up initially. This was especially true having regard to the commercial, technical and social environment of the 1970s. Passenger numbers were declining with the extension of car ownership and the growth of television, road congestion was becoming a noticeable feature of operation, staff recruitment and retention were increasingly difficult and expensive, the militancy which was to show itself later in the decade was just beginning and unreliability of the new rear-engined buses caused lost mileage at unacceptable levels.

In this situation the Executive found that most of its time was spent dealing with bus operating matters and was often 'fire fighting'. This meant that it had less time to deal with the wider issues for which PTAs/PTEs were established: namely making arrangements with other operators and land-use planning authorities and developing an integrated public transport network. The May 1972 proposals codified the Peter House (Head Office) organisation with three new appointments to the Executive Group. These were the appointment of AM (Angus) Munro as Chief Planning Officer; G Simpson as PRO and confirmed Jack Thompson as Controller of Integrated Operations (having taken up the role in December 1971) responsible for relationships with LUT, NBC and BR. Alderman George Mann became Chairman of the PTA.

Further the Executive decided, and the Authority approved, the 'hiving off' of the bus operation into a wholly-owned subsidiary, SELNEC Bus Holding Company Ltd. This was headed by a Managing Director, RLD (Richard) Cochrane, and supported by a Bus Board. This included Harry Taylor as Group Development Engineer and Peter Bland as Commercial Services Manager. Each of the three Divisions became bus companies: Northern Bus (SELNEC) Ltd, Central Bus (SELNEC) Ltd and Southern Bus (SELNEC) Ltd. Each was headed by a Chairman and Director/General Manager who were, respectively: David Graham and Jim Batty for the Northern Company; Ernest Armstrong and Norman Kay for Central and Geoff Harding and WB (Bill) Broadbent for the Southern. Norman Kay was translated from the Southern Division to replace Jack Thompson who had gone to Head Office and Bill Broadbent was a new appointment. He came from Staveley Industries and was a Crewe-trained apprentice. He was also connected with the Ffestiniog and Severn Valley Railways.

To complete the re-organisation, SELNEC Parcels became the SELNEC Parcels Express Company Ltd with Ken Freer as Managing Director. Its turnover was:

1969	£322,000
1970	£405,000
1971	£462,000

In January 1972 the Parcels Company moved from Hyde Road to Parrs Wood. It carried 8,000 parcels per day with a fleet of 40 vans and 100 staff. SELNEC Travel – the coaching subsidiary – eventually incorporated four fleets: Lancashire United, Godfrey Abbott, Charterplan and Warburtons.

1972 also saw a number of miscellaneous developments in the progress of SELNEC:
- the first two-door Leyland National, EX30, was delivered in May.
- a bus/train interchange at Great Moor Street in Bolton was approved in principle at a cost of £2.43m in July. (In fact this was never built since the design became so large it produced disbenefits to passengers!)
- in August an order for 500 buses including Leyland and Metro-Scania vehicles, was placed for delivery over the next 20 months. This order also included 4 Seddon Pennine midi-buses.
- the Picc-Vic scheme was approved in August at an estimated cost of £40m. This was to have been a full-sized railway tunnel underneath the City Centre linking Piccadilly station with Victoria station.
- In October SELNEC held its first Open Day at Hyde Rd garage and launched the film "A day in the life of SELNEC" with commentary by Michael Aspel.

In 1973 a programme of bus priority measure was begun, the biggest outside London. It started with a ¾mile stretch on both sides of Oxford Road from All Saints to the MRI (see opposite). The bus-only lane in-bound up

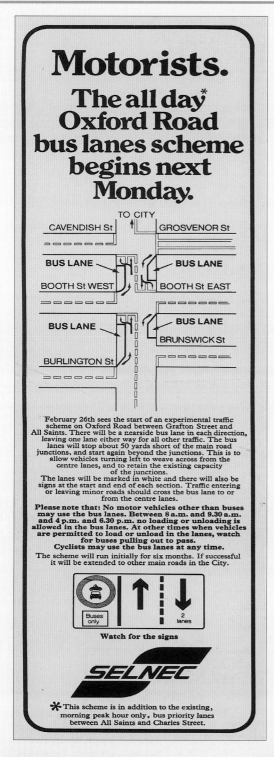

Motorists.
The all day* Oxford Road bus lanes scheme begins next Monday.

TO CITY

CAVENDISH St		GROSVENOR St
BUS LANE →		← BUS LANE
BOOTH St WEST		BOOTH St EAST
BUS LANE		BUS LANE
		BRUNSWICK St
BURLINGTON St		

February 26th sees the start of an experimental traffic scheme on Oxford Road between Grafton Street and All Saints. There will be a nearside bus lane in each direction, leaving one lane either way for all other traffic. The bus lanes will stop about 50 yards short of the main road junctions, and start again beyond the junctions. This is to allow vehicles turning left to weave across from the centre lanes, and to retain the existing capacity of the junctions.

The lanes will be marked in white and there will also be signs at the start and end of each section. Traffic entering or leaving minor roads should cross the bus lane to or from the centre lanes.

Please note that: No motor vehicles other than buses may use the bus lanes. Between 8 a.m. and 9.30 a.m. and 4 p.m. and 6.30 p.m. no loading or unloading is allowed in the bus lanes. At other times when vehicles are permitted to load or unload in the lanes, watch for buses pulling out to pass.

Cyclists may use the bus lanes at any time.

The scheme will run initially for six months. If successful it will be extended to other main roads in the City.

Watch for the signs

Buses only | 2 lanes

SELNEC

✱ This scheme is in addition to the existing, morning peak hour only, bus priority lanes between All Saints and Charles Street.

OTHER OPERATORS

Also providing bus services in the SELNEC area were Lancashire United Transport (LUT) based in Atherton; Ribble Motor Services (RMS) based in Preston, and the North Western Road Car Co Ltd (NWRC) based in Stockport. The latter two companies were part of the newly-formed National Bus Company (NBC), which had also been established as a result of the Transport Act 1968. There was also A Mayne and Son Ltd, whose garage was in Ashton New Road from where 29 buses and coaches were operated.

LUT was the largest independent bus company in Britain with 375 buses. R (Robert) Bailey was the General Manager. It had a turnover of £1.435m and operated 6.8m vehicle miles. Within the SELNEC area it had two garages: Atherton with 139 vehicles and Swinton with 153. Of its operations, 73% were internal to SELNEC.

Ribble's bus activities were concentrated in the north west of Manchester and Bolton although its express coach network radiated in all directions. It operated 1,267m vehicle miles from two depots in the area: Bolton with 38 vehicles and Bury with eight. G (George) Brook was the General Manager.

North Western's head office was in Charles Street, Stockport and GR (Robert) Brook was General Manager. The company had been founded in 1923 and operated in the counties of Cheshire, Lancashire, Derbyshire, Staffordshire and the West Riding of Yorkshire, garages being based in all but the latter county. NWRC had a turnover of £2m and operated 7.24m miles, 61% of it, and by far the most remunerative part, in the SELNEC area. The fleet was based at 13 garages, seven of which were within the SELNEC area based at Altrincham, Glossop, Oldham, Stockport, Urmston, Manchester and Wilmslow, all but the last two eventually passing to SELNEC.

It can thus be seen that SELNEC had the lion's share of bus operations on its area (75m vehicle miles to 15.3m) and was, therefore, in a strong position to consolidate the operations of the other operators. However, the route patterns of these companies, especially NWRC, made route simplification and rationalisation very difficult to achieve on paper, let alone commercially. Furthermore, these internal bus services were profitable and, with the possible exception of LUT, were cross-subsidising the Ribble and North Western services outside SELNEC so that the companies were unwilling to relinquish them without a fight and substantial payment.

One of Ribble's Alexander-bodied Atlanteans bound for Clitheroe stands in the former Lower Mosley Street bus station, now the site of the Bridgewater Hall. (DSH)

Negotiations With NBC

eanwhile negotiations continued between the PTE (led by Messrs Harrison, Graham and Thompson) and the National Bus company (represented by George Brook, now Regional Director and Robert Brook (no relation, but often confused!) of NWRC). From the early days of the PTE it became clear that if integration of bus routes was to be achieved, especially in the south of the SELNEC area, NWRC would have to be acquired. The official policy of NBC seemed to be opposed to selling off or breaking up any of its subsidiaries. However, by skilful negotiation the PTE was able to persuade the NBC to allow SELNEC to purchase NWRC, the deal being finally completed in 1972.

Selnec Cheshire

he actual mechanics by which this was achieved was that in December 1971 the NWRC routes would be split between SELNEC, Trent Motor Traction and Crosville. A new company was formed: North Western Road Car Co (SELNEC) Ltd. The transfer of garages, various properties, vehicles, and licences was completed by March 1972. NWRCCo (SELNEC) Ltd was then purchased by the SELNEC Cheshire Bus Company, whose vehicles now displayed the SELNEC symbol with a brown flash. Charles Street, Stockport continued to be the Head Office of the new subsidiary with TA (Tom) Dunstan being promoted from Traffic Manager to Director/General Manager.

North Western's York Street, Glossop, depot in SELNEC days with a Marshall-bodied Bristol RE bus, the Alexander-bodied Reliance shown opposite now also downgraded to bus work, and one of the AEC Renowns which latterly formed the exclusive double-deck allocation here. (JAS)

Above: The Renown deliveries were mixed in with Daimler Fleetlines with Alexander low height bodywork. DDB167C was one of a batch of 15 delivered in 1965, following 35 delivered in 1963 and 1964. A further 14 would follow in the following year. It is seen at the back of Charles Street garage. Some passed to Crosville. (JAS)

Number 326, a sister vehicle to the view on page 61, but now sporting the SELNEC sunglow orange and off-white livery, together with the brown SELNEC Cheshire flash. The vehicle looks much more attractive to the passenger. It is seen here laying over at the Hazel Grove (Rising Sun) terminus, before departing on the hilly and winding cross-country route through Marple to Glossop. *(DSH)*

Former North Western 833, now in SELNEC Cheshire livery. The Alexander Highway semi-coach body looks good and belies its age when photographed. It is based on an AEC Reliance chassis. Delivered originally in 1961 as a coach, re-designated dual-purpose in 1966 and further cascaded in 1968 to a service bus. Photographed here in 1972 on Glossop Railway Station forecourt before departing for Simmondley. *(JAS)*

A Bristol VR/ECW, 413 delivered new to SELNEC Cheshire, seen here at the Wellington Road Bus Park in Stockport. Twenty five of these buses had been ordered by NWRC before the break-up and purchase of part of the company by SELNEC. There was just sufficient time to get ECW to produce the standard SELNEC destination layout at the front and side number blind above the downstairs front window. This handsome body looks even better in the pristine SELNEC livery. *(DSH)*

FORMER NWRC

Former North Western vehicles continued to be seen in Manchester, quite apart from those which had passed to SELNEC. Looking quite smart and standing out from the by-now all-pervading Orange and White is ex-NWRC 212, an Alexander-bodied low-height Fleetline now repainted in the colours of Crosville Motor Services and loading at Parker Street Bus Station, Piccadilly, Manchester on the former NWRC service via Wilmslow to Macclesfield. This is one of the vehicles working on a route passed to Crosville when the original NWRC organisation was split. *(JAS)*

Another vehicle passed from former NWRC to Crosville, this time a Leyland Leopard/Alexander 'Y' type coach in the dual-purpose livery adopted by its new owner. and working the 842 service to Blackpool. Crosville also gained Dennis Lolines and Bristol REs whilst Trent received a share of former North Western vehicles. *(STA)*

The then newly-introduced universal all-white livery for National coaches, with its miniscule fleetname above the wheelarch, is perhaps one of the best examples of the inadvisability of letting people who don't use public transport anywhere near decision making which affects the travelling public. Former North Western SJA404K awaits departure for Manchester from Buxton on the X5B service. *(STA)*

LANCASHIRE UNITED

Route Exchanges

At their meeting on 21st June 1973, SELNEC PTA agreed a programme of bus route exchanges in the north and west of the conurbation. This followed on from the PTE's agreement with LUT and the on-going discussions with NBC. Some routes were to be transferred from Ribble to LUT and/or SELNEC Northern. Other routes were to be transferred from LUT and SELNEC Northern to Ribble or Crosville. In some cases in the second group there was joint operation with LUT and Warrington Corporation. Also in this category were many of Lancashire Pool and Tyne-Tees-Mersey services. As a number of Objections were made to these proposals a hearing before the Traffic Commissioners had to be held and the date of that was set for 26th March 1974. The revenue earned and the mileage operated just about balanced out, although there were detailed differences in other costs. In due course the Traffic Commissioner approved these complex proposals.

The first agreement was signed with LUT in January 1971 under which LUT continued to operate their services on a cost-plus basis. The PTE paid LUT the cost of its mileage plus a sum for managing the services and to give them a reasonable return on capital. This agreement replaced previously long-standing agreements between the Company and Salford, Bolton and Leigh Corporations. At a stroke the agreement reduced the complications of joint working and the clerical work in balancing mileage and revenue. It also allowed LUT's fares to be brought in-line with SELNEC's fares and facilitated the exchange of routes. The agreement also gave the PTE the option to acquire the Company.

Posed outside the former trolleybus depot and in front of the old power station at Atherton, both reminders of the South Lancashire Transport Company, Lancashire United's number 412, VTC502M, a 33ft long 'JUMBO' double-decker has just been delivered from Northern Counties factory in Wigan in 1974. Engineer Graham Dewhurst was keen to show off his latest acquisition, though there would be only one more of these vehicles before the Standards shown overleaf took over in 1977. These dual-door buses seated 49 upstairs and 27 in the lower saloon. LUT elected to take the longer wheelbase Fleetline CRG6LXB chassis which Manchester had also used under its Daimler Mancunians. The PTE opted for the shorter 30ft model because of its greater ease of manoeuvrability. The enclosed rear engine compartment is noteworthy. (JAS)

The **LUT** fleet, like its operating area, was large and varied. With a backdrop of one of the last mill chimneys in the area, alongside the mill buildings, one of its many single-deckers pauses to wait for passengers just outside Atherton. Number 390 is one of 50 Seddon Pennine RUs, dating from 1971 and fitted with Plaxton bodywork, all of which passed to GMT in 1976. *(JAS)*

Swinton Church provides the background for this shot of two of LUT's front-engined double-deck fleet, 272 a Northern Counties-bodied Guy Arab V and a Metro-Cammell bodied Arab IV. There were also Daimler Fleetlines, again bodied by NCME. The A6 trunk road to Chorley and Blackpool to the left, and Manchester to the right, crosses at the traffic lights in the middle distance.

The fleet also included dual-purpose vehicles and coaches, the latter eventually standardised on Leyland Leopards with Plaxton bodywork. Here preserved example No. 216 dating from 1966 is seen outside Boyle Street at an LUT running day. *(JAS both)*

LUT STANDARDS – BEGINNING OF THE END

Lancashire United managed to remain some of its individuality until the last of its former bespoke vehicles was withdrawn, a Plaxton-bodied Leopard delivered new in 1978.

On January 1st 1976 the PTE exercised its option to purchase the company and vehicle purchasing now became to GMT standard policy. However, even when Fleetline Standards were allocated to the former independent, the first examples arrived in LUT's red and grey livery, and their seats were trimmed with LUT moquette rather than GMT orange and brown. Final integration of this charismatic operator took place in 1978. In that year it received seven Leyland Nationals in London Transport red, its own house red not being available from Workington, of course.

When corporate livery gradually came in, it was applied to the fleet in various guises, none of which matched the rest of the fleet.

LUT Standard 485 stands on the forecourt at Northern Counties Wigan Lane factory in 1977, posed for a photograph for the history of Northern Counties bodybuilding activities then in progress. It was the first such vehicle delivered to LUT whilst under GMT ownership, a landmark of sorts. The LUT livery fitted in well with the clean lines of the new body design. It would later be renumbered 6901.

Preserved example 6990, formerly LUT 613, was the last LUT Standard, delivered in 1980 and is seen moving through Heaton Park for a very wet Trans-Lancs rally. It shows the application of the GMT orange and white livery to former LUT double-deckers whilst below the two versions of the logo – the M-blem – can be seen. (JAS all)

FURTHER REORGANISATION

In March 1973 the consultants Urwick, Orr and Partners Ltd tabled their draft report on the revised organisation of the Executive and, in particular, its bus operations. By this time the Executive had three years' experience of its responsibilities; it had acquired North Western and integrated its operations, it had made a cost-plus agreement with LUT with an option to purchase, it had made agreements with NBC and BR and was paying the latter substantial sums of money. Furthermore, it was becoming clear that the free-standing PTA would be replaced by the Greater Manchester Metropolitan County Council (GMCC) within a year, which would bring in the buses of Wigan Corporation. One of the criticisms of the then current organisation was that there were too many tiers in it – there was a need to delegate decisions to individuals rather than committees or working parties.

There was to be one Executive Committee – replacing the previous Corporate Management Group and Bus Board – consisting of four Directors and the senior functional Executives/Managers. Tony Harrison and David Graham continued as DG and Director of Finance, respectively, and were joined by Angus Munro as Director of Planning. Geoff Harding moved to become Director of Research and Development and Ernest Armstrong retired. Ian Buttress continued as Secretary. Other members of the Executive Committee were: Corporate Services Manager (Richard Cochrane), Chief Marketing Executive (Peter Evans), Controller of Integrated Operations (Jack Thompson), Chief Operations Executive (Bill Broadbent), and Chief Personnel Executive (Colin Howarth). The newcomers were Peter Evans who joined from Shell and Colin Howarth who had carried out the study for Urwick, Orr.

In operational terms these changes, fully implemented by early 1974, were significant. The seven District Managers answered to the District's Operations Manager, who was Jim Batty. Thus the Southern and Northern Bus companies disappeared. Each of the three areas in the Central Company, NW, E and S, became Divisions in their own right, each headed by a Divisional General Manager. The new DGMs were: Mike Hicks for Central NW, Tom Dunstan for Central Southern and John Marsh for Central Eastern based, respectively, at Frederick Road, Princess Road and Hyde Road garages. The re-organised Bus Board under Bill Broadbent also included a Chief Operations Engineer (Brian Holcroft), a Services Manager (Operations) (Ken Holt), a Works Study Manager (Jim Kinnell) and an Operational Control Accountant (Ron Fowles). Because of the difference in size of the Divisions/Districts there were local variations in internal organisation. Also of major consequence to the future was the Chief Marketing Executive who had a Services Manager (Marketing). This post was filled by DR (Denis) Rodgers, who had been the Traffic Manager at LUT. It was also a sign of the times that the Chief Personnel Executive had individual Industrial Relations Managers for each of the main Trade Union groups: TGWU, NALGO, ACTSS, etc. One of these was Cyril Burton, IRO (TGWU), a very able traffic man.

Two significant retirements took place in 1975. First Bob Bailey, Director and General Manager of LUT, retired after 46 years' service in the bus industry and 11 years at LUT. On leaving LUT, Bob became Commercial Services Executive at the PTE and Chairman of several subsidiary companies. His place was taken by KE (Ken) Holt who had worked his way up through Manchester City Transport. The second was the retirement of W (Bill) Mitchell, District Manager at Leigh. Bill was a Cornishman who never lost his accent in spite of arriving in Lancashire in 1953, when he joined Leigh Corporation as Traffic Superintendent. He rose to become Deputy General Manager and then General Manager in 1969.

With the establishment of the two new PTEs in Yorkshire, it was inevitable that a number of SELNEC personnel would be appointed to senior positions the other side of the Pennines. Norman Kay went to become the Director of Operations and Planning at South Yorkshire PTE in Sheffield – later becoming Director General. He was joined by Len Trueman, who became Director of Personnel at that PTE. John Clarkson left SELNEC to become Director of Finance and Administration at West Yorkshire PTE, then based in Wakefield. He was joined by Harry Taylor who became Director of Engineering.

RAILWAYS IN SELNEC'S AREA

– Lancashire & Yorkshire; London & North Western; Great Central; Midland Railway and Cheshire Lines Committee – had provided services from five separate terminal stations: Victoria, Exchange, Central, Oxford Road and London Road (renamed Piccadilly in 1960). The 1966 journey-to-work survey showed that SELNEC's railways were the heaviest used of the four original PTEs, carrying around 15m passengers per annum.

Two of the reasons for developing PTEs were the publication in the early 1960s of the Buchanan Report 'Traffic in Towns' and the Beeching Plan for the 'Reshaping of British Railways'. The former stressed the importance of public transport and the latter proposed extensive railway closures unless local authorities were prepared to support them financially.

Manchester had been at the heart of railway development since the opening of the Liverpool & Manchester Railway in 1820. At its height five railways

Dwarfed by the mass of gantries and the associated wiring for the southbound 25kv electric trains, and further to the left the 1500v dc lines to the east, an early Derby Lightweight set makes a smokey exit on its journey to New Mills Central. The future of the whole of the local railway network was under review as explained in the text on the opposite page. *(JAS)*

BEECHING CLOSURES

In November 1969 there were 25 services operating, of which seven were internal to the SELNEC area. The remaining 18 were cross-boundary. PTEs had to have regard to places 25 miles beyond their boundary and there was a location near Crewe that could be influenced by three PTEs! The complete list of services is set out in the table on page 76. Of these, five were already slated for closure under the Beeching Plan, they were:

New Mills Central – Hayfield
Romiley – Macclesfield
Rochdale – Bury – Bolton
Bury – Rawtenstall
Oldham – Rochdale

To assess the future potential of these five and the other 25 services, the SELNEC Transportation Study was used to evaluate them against a variety of land-use and other factors. Suffice it to say that none of them passed muster. However, from economic, social and political perspectives there was great reluctance to close the Oldham-Rochdale line and it has struggled on for 40 years and now will be incorporated into the Metrolink network. (Talk about persistence!) The other four lines were closed in 1970, although the line to Macclesfield was only closed from Marple Rose Hill after a successful campaign to retain the service from Rose Hill to Manchester through Romiley. The Bury-Rawtenstall line was closed in 1972 (subsequently to be taken over by the East Lancashire Railway Preservation Society). The closure of Bury Bolton Street eventually enabled the tracks to be slewed to an alignment which allowed Bury Interchange to be built in Kay Gardens. In 1972 regular service on the Stockport – Stalybridge service was withdrawn though the statutory one-train-per-week still runs every Friday afternoon at the time of writing.

Manchester Central Station closed on 5th May 1969 and subsequently, and much later, became the G-Mex Exhibition Centre – only to later be renamed Manchester Central once more! Trains using it were diverted to Victoria or Oxford Road. In 1958, as part of the West Coast Main Line electrification, the Manchester, South Junction and Altrincham (MSJA) service had been cut back from London Road (now Piccadilly) to Oxford Road whilst 25kV electrification was extended through platforms 13 & 14 at Piccadilly to Oxford Road. In 1971 the MJSA was converted from 1500v DC to 25kV AC electrification and the Altrincham line services were linked through to those running to Alderley Edge and Crewe. The original 1931 sets were scrapped and replaced by Class AM4s (now 304) EMUs.

After much analysis and deliberation SELNEC took over responsibility for planning and financing the local train services on 1st January 1972, under Section 20 of the Transport Act 1968. The cost of support in 1969 was £5.035m. It has to be remembered that at this time bus operations were profitable. In effect there were two rail networks in Manchester: a northern one based on Victoria and a southern one based on Piccadilly. The northern services were DMU-operated, except for the Bury line which was worked by 2-car EMUs operating on the unique third rail 1200v DC side-contact system. In 1992 the Bury line became part of the Metrolink system. The southern network was also diesel-operated except for the MSJA, to which reference has just been made, and the Alderley Edge/Crewe via both Stockport and Styal services operated by 25kV AC electrified EMUs (Class 304).

The Hadfield/Glossop service was also operated at 1500v DC overhead with 57ft long 3-car EMUs (Class 506) designed by the LNER. In December 1984 this service was converted to 25kV AC electrification. Former 'Blue Train' stock cascaded from the Glasgow area then took over the operation. Unfortunately the 61ft 6in stock was too long to allow two sets of three cars to work in multiple at rush hours and consequently the capacity of the replacement trains at peak periods was only half that of the old stock they replaced. It was not considered to be a great improvement by those who could actually get on to stand on their way home.

1	2 ANNUAL SOCIAL GRANT per service £'000		3 No. of passenger (wkday double trip)	4 SOCIAL GRANT per passenger per year £'000		5 COSTS £'000					6 Total Costs £'000	7 Earnings £'000	8 Passenger Miles 000	9 Costs per passenger mile (d)	10 Deficit per passenger mile (d)
SERVICE	BASIS 'A'	BASIS 'B'		BASIS 'A'	BASIS 'B'	A Movement	B Terminal	C Track & Signalling	D Interest	E Administration				(d)	(d)
WHOLLY WITHIN AREA															
Or/Altrincham	338		9080	36.5		231	102	163	67	46	609	271	23,887	6.410	3.717
Rochdale/Bury/Bolton	179		840	213.0		53	50	83	11	13	210	31	2,903	17.360	14.800
Vic/Oldham/Rochdale	438		2300	190.0		128	89	220	32	28	497	59	6,868	17.236	15.306
Stockport/Stalybridge	100		333	300.0		33	23	51	7	7	121	21	1,770	16.406	13.559
Vic/Bury	373		5372	69.4		139	95	222	53	32	541	168	16,034	8.128	5.673
Pic/Glossop/Hayfield	288		1970	146.2		86	45	167	47	17	362	74	8,223	11.115	9.078
Pic/New Mills	344		5000	68.8		202	80	440	36	37	513	169	18,553	6.237	4.223
SUB TOTAL	2,060		24895										78,238		
PARTLY WITHIN AREA															
Vic/Bolton/Preston/B'pool	160	290	3,870	41.3	74.9	504	185	400	75	103	1,267	538	61,271	1.970	2.460
Or/Warrington/Liverpool	130	300	6,729	19.3	44.6	389	161	372	77	72	1,071	581	59,368	4.702	2.394
Leeds/M'cr/Liverpool	90	70	2,150	41.9	32.6	272	76	250	41	52	691	442	42,793	1.530	1.120
Or/Warrington/Chester	20	130	2,900	6.9	44.9	191	50	120	27	36	424	195	20,935	2.190	2.190
Or/Northwich/Chester	90	150	2,945	30.6	50.9	210	90	153	33	39	525	241	25,103	5.545	3.336
Pic/Stoke/Stafford	230	270	5,923	38.8	45.6	267	157	349	128	58	959	386	46,421	5.139	3.138
Pic/Derby	67		430	155.8		233	27	105	43	30	438	222	22,369	2.500	2.564
Pic/Buxton	290	140	3,850	75.3	36.3	230	87	199	51	42	609	225	24,500	6.122	4.055
Bury/Rawtenstall	110	90	420	261.9	214.3	29	8	87	0	5	139	9	1,056	32.500	30.000
Or/Styal/Crewe	290	280	3,350	86.6	83.6	94	51	186	58	20	409	110	12,445	8.060	6.090
Or/Stockport/Crewe	310	270	5,150	60.2	52.4	185	121	251	86	41	684	265	26,900	6.250	3.990
Vic/Bolton/Blackburn/Colne	225		2,870	78.4		270	130	328	53	52	833	176	18,592	10.792	8.598
Vic/Patricroft/Liverpool	20	50	1,088	18.4	45.9	55	40	42	10	13	160	47	3,134	6.203	4.059
Vic/Huddersfield	60	70	985	61.0	71.1	44	38	41	9	11	143	56	5,359	6.381	3.882
Vic/Wigan/Southport	280	360	4,000	70.0	90.0	315	127	461	83	59	1,045	314	33,908	7.474	5.273
Pic/Sheffield (via Hope Valley)	33					7	2	14	2	1	26	9	712	2.360	3.030
Vic/Bradford	120	130													
Bolton/Wigan/Liverpool	70	50													
SUB TOTAL	2,595	2,975	46,660										404,866		
GRAND TOTAL	4,655	5,035	71,555										483,104		

Notes: BASIS 'A' based on passenger mileage.
BASIS 'B' based on 'Costs and Earnings where they fall' formula.

BR's Class 506 3-car EMU's were designed by the LNER before World War II for the Manchester-Glossop/Hadfield suburban service which was inaugurated in September 1954, having been delayed by the war. The EMU's were similar to those built for the Liverpool Street-Shenfield electrification, inaugurated about the same time. Some of the EMU's were built by Birmingham Railway Carriage and Wagon Co., some of the others by Metropolitan-Cammell. Eight EMU's were allocated to the Glossop/Hadfield service. In December 1984 the DC system ceased and the Class 506 units were scrapped and the line was converted to 25kV AC operation. *(JAS both)*

Although photographed in Wilmslow station on the Styal line platforms, this former Glasgow Blue Train 25 kV AC EMU 303048, had been cascaded to Manchester to serve the Glossop/Hadfield service, converted to AC operation in December 1984. It is seen here working a Wilmslow-Altrincham service, before the Airport spur was built. The Class 303 units had been built by the Pressed Steel Company for the inauguration of the Clydeside Electric services in 1960. In many respects they were an updated version of the Glossop/Hadfield units, but with a more stylish front end. Their increased length had apparently not been considered when the change was made, as described on the previous page. *(APY)*

The Metro-Cammell diesel multiple units, later branded class 101, became the most successful and longest surviving units on BR and finished their days working out of Manchester Piccadilly. Here a set in mixed livery in the 1970s passes through Agecroft, *en route* to Victoria. The cooling towers of the erstwhile Agecroft power station can be seen in the background. *(JAS)*

Below: The BRCW stock used on the Manchester to Buxton line was always noteworthy for the white cab roof ends, though just why they were so painted seems to be a mystery. A three car Buxton-bound set emerges from the short Doveholes tunnel near Chapel-en-le-Frith. *(JAS)*

3-car EMU built by Metropolitan Cammell Carriage & Wagon Co. for the electrification of the Manchester South Junction and Altrincham Railway. The electric service started on 11th May 1931, with 6-car trains being operated in the peak. During World War II 7-car trains were tried but did not prove satisfactory in blackout conditions. Twenty-two set were built and this one, M28588M, was 39 years old when photographed in the bay platform at Oxford Road. (DSH)

Oxford Road Station, with the famous tower of the Refuge Insurance building in the background, was rebuilt in 1958 when the MSJA service was cut back from London Road (now named Piccadilly) in connection with the Manchester/Liverpool-Crewe electrification. Originally there were two bay platforms for the terminating MSJA service, but by the time this photo was taken, one had been removed. A 3-car MSJA EMU awaits is departure. In the adjacent platform is a 25kV AC 4-car EMU (Type AM4, subsequently Class 304) ready to depart towards Piccadilly before journeying southwards. (JAS)

A 4-car Type AM4 EMU arriving on Platform 13 at Piccadilly Station with an Altrincham-Crewe working. In 1971 the MSJA was converted to 25 kV AC operation, although many of the overhead gantries and wiring were retained, only being replaced in the major Matrolink upgrade of 2009. The new AC units were slower than their predecessor DC units on the Altrincham line, but linking services round the south side of Manchester probably meant that overall journey times were little changed. (APY)

Altrincham station in heavy rail days with a Type AM4, 4-car EMU waiting in platform 4 ready for departure to Manchester and onwards. Now the southern terminus of Metrolink, the station awnings and footbridge remained little altered other than for a repaint! *(APY)*

Oxford Road station looking eastwards towards the two-track section to Piccadilly. A Type AM4 unit (031) is departing *en route* to Crewe via Stockport. Similar type of units, but in 2-car form and for DC traction, also operated the Victoria-Bury service. This intensively used section carries freight, Trans-Pennine and long distance express services and is signalled for bi-directional working. *(JAS)*

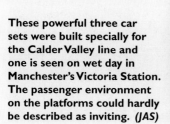

These powerful three car sets were built specially for the Calder Valley line and one is seen on wet day in Manchester's Victoria Station. The passenger environment on the platforms could hardly be described as inviting. *(JAS)*

The Picc-Vic Project

To link the separate rail networks and to improve central area penetration for passengers SELNEC was planning the cross-city underground railway link between Piccadilly Station and Victoria (the Picc-Vic scheme). Many alternative alignments and station locations were evaluated by the Transportation Study, but the route for which Parliamentary Powers were obtained in 1972 was to be a link 2.75 miles long of which 2.18 miles were in tunnel and have intermediate underground stations at Whitworth Street/Princess Street, Albert Square and Royal Exchange. There would also have been low-level stations at Piccadilly and Victoria. It was hoped to open the tunnel in 1977/78 when a 2½ minute peak and a 7½ minute off-peak service would have been run through, connecting Bolton with Wilmslow via Styal, Bury via Stockport to Alderley Edge; Victoria to Hazel Grove and Victoria to Macclesfield. The PTA approved the scheme in August 1972 at a cost of £40m. At later stages it was hoped to extend the Victoria terminating trains to Rochdale direct and via Oldham. Hazel Grove terminating services could have also been extended to Buxton,

and discussions had taken place with Derbyshire County Council. Services would have been operated by 3-car EMUs, either of BR's PEP stock design or a Metro-Cammell design. Unfortunately the economic circumstances of the day led to the government withdrawing support for the scheme in August 1973. For the next four years, encouraged by continuing support from SELNEC PTA and Greater Manchester Council, the PTE developed numerous rephasings and simplifications – but to no avail. With a change of local Political control in 1977, the scheme was abandoned and the Parliamentary Powers lapsed.

As with all things, railway timescales are much longer than dealing with buses, largely because of infrastructure issues. Much time and resource of the PTE's Planning Department was put into working with the Transportation Study, evaluating the railway network and devising ways of operating it more economically and evaluating bus/train/car interchange sites. Few of these came to fruition during the SELNEC period, except for a large car park at Cheadle Hulme. However, the seeds were sown for Interchanges at Altrincham, Bury, Whitefield and Hazel Grove, and eleven new stations opened in the early 1980s. The Bolton scheme, mentioned earlier, was dropped in favour of a simpler scheme at Trinity Street.

By 1974 the cost of supporting the 20 local services was £11,976m, of which the PTE had to pay £6,203m. These costs and apportionments were calculated on a formula developed by Cooper Brothers, the Chartered Accountants. Following Britain's membership of the EEC the calculation of support altered in 1974 into a block grant system.

An artist's impression of how the station at Royal Exchange might have looked. *(MMoT)*

GREATER MANCHESTER METROPOLITAN COUNTY COUNCIL

The reform of local government in England and Wales had been on the agenda for governments for some time. The Redcliffe-Maude Commission proposed Unitary authorities to cover the larger urban agglomerations, but there was considerable resistance to these proposals.

With the change of government the idea of conurbation – wide councils for the largest metropolitan areas – then found favour. However, Barbara Castle, as Minister of Transport, said that the transport problems of these areas were too urgent to wait the wholesale re-organisation of local government. Accordingly she pressed ahead with establishing the original four PTA/PTEs.

The Local Government Act 1972 came into effect on 1st April 1974. It established the Greater Manchester Metropolitan County Council (GMMC) based on Westminster House, subsequently to become County Hall, in Portland Street, Manchester. The first Chief Executive was Sir George Ogden, who had previously been the Town Clerk and Chief Executive of the City of Manchester. The role of SELNEC PTA was taken over by the Highways & Transportation Committee, which met monthly. Officially the role of the Executive did not change, but its freedoms were subtly constrained in numerous ways.

The organisation introduced by the Executive the previous year stood it in good stead. The SELNEC name was replaced by Greater Manchester Transport and the 'double M' symbol. (MM had been conceived as being Manchester metro, but somehow this idea never saw the light of day.) The colour-scheme remained the same to all-intents-and-purposes, but aficionados noted that the previous off-white became a more brilliant white. The route re-numbering had been completed by this point. During its short life SELNEC had taken delivery of 908 buses and withdrawn 968 from the inherited municipal fleets.

Wigan County Borough became the Metropolitan district of Wigan within the GMMC and the Corporation's buses (114 d/d and 16 s/ds) were transferred into the Northern Division of GM Buses. Wigan Corporation had a combined garage and workshop at Melverley

With the inclusion of the Wigan fleet in 1974, following the boundary changes mentioned in the text, the SELNEC vehicle empire reached its maximum size. The fleet was all-Leyland, with bodywork either by Massey or Northern Counties, both builders being based in the town. The four double-deckers shown below were typical of the front engined fleet, Leyland PD2 or PD3s with attractive Massey bodywork. There were also 32 Northern Counties-bodied Atlanteans at the time of the takeover. One of the forward entrance PD2 examples survived in the driver training fleet for many years whilst another of the same type passed into preservation at Boyle Street. Number 114, last in this line up, is also kept in pristine condition at the Manchester Museum of Transport. *(APY)*

Street. RMC (Max) Baschy, the General Manager, became the District Manager. However, at the other end of the SELNEC area, Wilmslow and Poynton reverted to Cheshire County Council, following much lobbying to do so, and Glossop reverted to Derbyshire County Council. The name SELNEC survived only in connection with the Parcels Express Company and SELNEC Travel, the coaching business.

In mid-1976 Sir George Ogden retired as the Chief Executive of GMMC and Tony Harrison was appointed to the post. David Graham stepped up to become Director General of GMPTE and DC (Des) Holley became the PTE's Director of Finance on 17th August. Jim Batty finally got the top bus operating job, becoming Director of Operations for GMPTE on 7th August 1976, with 'JT' – Jack Thompson being elevated to Director of Integrated Operations and responsible for all non-direct bus operations and railways.

In 1985/6 the Greater Manchester bus operation carried 350m passengers, with the bus and coach fleet operating 88,520m miles. The total fleet was 2,987 buses, of which 2,400 were double-deckers and 587 were single-deckers. There were 7,288 staff operating from 27 depots. There were 10 bus stations/interchanges and 12,000 individual bus stops. In addition the Executive were responsible for 23 railway services, covering a route-network of 159.39 miles and 113 stations.

The Greater Manchester Transport story is an interesting one to be told hopefully at another time, and lasted until 26th October 1986, when deregulation and privatisation came long under the Transport Act 1985. GM Buses was then split into two limited companies: GM Buses North, based on Queens Road and GM Buses South, based on Stockport. In due course, and after considerable resistance from the GMPTA, these companies were sold to First and Stagecoach respectively. But, as they say – that, too, is another story!

With the change to GM Buses there were yet more livery styles, with the emphasis on the strong orange colour being retained, and, as here, increased through a revised application. Sunglow Orange and Mancunian White had given way to GMT Orange and GMT White as the officially designated colours but more changes would follow over the years and after the formation of the two companies. Examples of the different schemes can be seen at the open days and rallies held in the area when buses preserved and housed at the Museum of Transport in Cheetham Hill rub shoulders with the many examples from the SELNEC Preservation Society's fleet. (JAS)

31/10/09